FLANDR[E]
BOULONNAIS
ARTOIS
PICARDIE
COTENTIN
CAUX
CHAMPAGNE
LORRAINE
NORMANDIE
ILE-DE-FRANCE
ALSACE
BRIE
VOSGES
BRETAGNE
MAINE
BEAUCE
ORLEANAIS
FRANCHE-COMTE
SOLONGE
BOURGOGNE
ANJOU
BERRY
TOURAINE
BOURBONNAIS
VENDEE
MARCHE
FOREZ
POITOU
LYONNAIS
LIMOUSIN
AUVERGNE
SAVOIE
PERIGORD
DAUPHINE
GEVAUDAN
GUYENNE
QUERCY
LANDES
PROVENCE
ARMAGNAC
LANGUEDOC
GASCOGNE
PAYS BASQUE
BEARN
ROUSSILLON

HISTORICAL REGIONS

The
French Farmhouse

Elsie Burch Donald

Illustrated by Csaba Pasztor

Photographs by the Author

LITTLE, BROWN AND COMPANY

Boston New York London Toronto

A LITTLE, BROWN BOOK

First published in Great Britain in 1995
by Little, Brown and Company (UK)

Conceived, written and edited by
Elsie Burch Donald

A CIP catalogue record for this book is
available from the British Library

ISBN 0-316-91226 3

Designed by Lawrence and Beavan
Typeset by Concept Communications Ltd
Colour reproduction, printing and binding
Mandarin Offset Ltd.

*Previous page: farmhouse
doorway with megalithic
granite lintel in the Grande
Brière (Brittany).*

Little, Brown and Company (UK)
Brettenham House
Lancaster Place
London WC2E 7EN

CONTENTS

AUTHOR'S NOTE

To live in a farmhouse in France, even for a few weeks, has become a favourite fantasy of the city dweller. Equally the prospect of restoring an old house, reviving a derelict ruin and turning it into the house of one's dreams causes many a heart to beat faster, longingly.

And such desires are increasingly within reach. As farms have grown larger in France the houses that were once attached to smallholdings are being sold and the buyers, usually city dwellers, are not often French: English, Dutch, Swiss, they can come from as far away as America and Hong Kong.

But as outsiders move in and restorations get underway; as cracked tiled floors are pulled up and the old stone sinks ripped out, as bathrooms are installed in *chais* and re-roofing begins, the face-lift is in danger of removing the hard-won lines of character – a character that is intimately if not, as it turns out, inextricably linked to France's peasant history. For every feature of these old houses, every niche and outbuilding, once had its *raison d'être* as a piece of efficiency to help the peasant produce his daily bread. Only rarely was it freshly-baked however or did sunlight fall across a comfortable farmhouse kitchen. Peasant life was a crowded, primitive affair and fresh-baked bread – like neat and comfortable homes – largely a dream.

But it is a dream that farmhouse owners today can realize and, in doing so, perhaps will crown the peasant's long and Sisyphean struggle – for if dreams come true others have not laboured in vain. If that is to happen however the facts round which such dreams were built must be made known, and not ignored. The function and purpose of peasant houses, their evolution and the life that was lived inside them must be told; for without it there is merely Disneyland.

In undertaking such a task this book is therefore, in addition to being a study of old farmhouses, a kind of biography.

Of the many who have helped in the book's preparation I particularly wish to thank Jane Dorrell for her diligent and efficient proofreading and Annick Stein, herself a journalist in this field in France, who gave unstinting help to a comparative stranger. The cooperation of Maisons Paysannes de France was instrumental in the book's becoming a reality and later indispensable in the technical vetting of the text.

I would also like to thank R H Bennett of the Lime Institute; G De Lunardo; Fearn King; J Le Ber; Ronald A Lee; Madame Magnier-Vazeilles, Fondation Marius-Vazeilles; Madame M L Mallard; Professor Gwyn Meirion-Jones; Claire Fons, librarian, Institut Francais; David Roberts, Berry Bros & Rudd and Dr M J Wilson, Macaulay Land Use Research Institute. I am grateful too for the repeated kindnesses I received from house owners during my research in France and I am indebted to the historians whose books guided me on my odyssey and whose names appear in the bibliography.

Finally, the subject is a big one and if readers are not to be confused by excessive detail then strong and absorbable patterns must be created, often at the expense of paler hues, and there is almost no statement in this book that does not have its exceptions.

Derelict Breton row houses possess a faded charm that, in appealing to the restorer, also begs restraint.

INTRODUCTION

The huge changes in French rural society since the 1950s have brought one great bonus for anyone wanting to buy a cottage, mansion or farmhouse: there are masses of them available, at very reasonable prices. The peasants in their millions have left the land for the towns, and their old homes are free for other uses.

For better or for worse – and I see it as largely for the better – various modern influences have transformed French agriculture and with it the lives of farmers and villagers. Farm mechanization has caused more than six million people to move off the land: farming's share of France's active population has dropped since 1945 from thirty-five to seven per cent and is falling still. Those who remain now have much larger farms and are far more prosperous; they have lost the old mentality of the *paysan* and are now more like businessmen, obsessed by modern techniques of production and marketing. Thus the old gulf between town and country has narrowed, and the old-style peasant is a dying breed. Horses, ploughs and oxen are replaced by tractors and big cars; colour TV, the video, Minitel and deep-freeze have invaded the old farmstead home. The traditional costumes are no longer in daily use, but are worn just by folk-groups at fêtes.

All this may be a blow for folksy picturesqueness. But there are compensations. The new French, in a new style, are eager to preserve and rediscover their rural heritage. Little groups of enthusiasts have been reviving the old folk-dances and musical instruments, even some of the local country crafts and the dying regional languages. In summer, there are local arts festivals everywhere. And many of the old rural buildings have been lovingly restored. True, there are some new eyesores: but mostly the rural habitat and the villages have kept their old outward looks and aura, despite the very different new society and life-styles that they now contain.

And what a marvellous heritage it is, in this beautiful, spacious, hugely diverse land, where tradition varies so much from region to region, even within regions – in rural architecture as in cuisine, folklore, political habits. France to the world may present a strong unified personality but in fact Frenchness wears not one but a thousand faces. The historian Fernand Braudel, in his work The Identity of France, concluded that its identity was indefinable, the sum of its myriad parts.

One clue to this rich diversity is that France is the only country — bar Russia — that belongs both to north and south Europe. The grey granite cottages of Celtic Brittany, austere but dignified, are in another civilisation from the Mediterranean world of Provence or Languedoc, where walled red-roofed villages cling to hilltops and old men play boules in shady squares. And between these extremes are many other local styles, dictated often by climate, soil or building materials locally available — the half-timbered facades of Normandy, repeated in a different form in Alsace; the alpine chalets of Savoy; the handsome low brick farmsteads of the Sologne plain; the galleried houses of Burgundy vignerons where the first floor is the main room; the stark, squat buildings of upland Auvergne and in contrast the cheerful flower-decked red-and-white villages of the Basques.

The various styles somehow relate to local character: so the rural architecture of France is the visual panorama of a civilisation. And within the houses, local styles of furniture and decor vary, too — from the carved oak chests and box-beds of Brittany to the red tiled floors and bead curtains of Provence.

Today, middle-class newcomers from the towns — mostly from Paris or abroad — have taken over many of the rural buildings. They use them as holiday or retirement homes; or they bring their jobs with them, to work in the country as artists, writers, craftsmen, even engineers. They have given the dying villages a new vibrant life. Often it is these immigrants who have taken the lead in tastefully restoring the old country buildings.

Another trend is that much of the newer post-war building keeps to the old local styles. Everywhere in Provence you'll find new villas and hotels with the traditional red-tiled roofs, white walls and patios; Alsatians and Normans are still attached to half-timbering; and the new cottages along Brittany's coasts stick more-or-less to the sober grey Breton styles. This mock-vernacular may lack the grace and patina of the originals but it is yet another sign of the French concern today to keep faith with their much-loved rural traditions.

John Ardagh

THE LAND

The central fact of peasant life was land. Not only was it the source of food but clothing and household furnishings came from it, and all of the materials for building. Every part of a house: its walls, roof, floors, the joists and mortar were products of the soil, laboriously transformed by hands and sweat to a desired end; and this continued to be so in parts of France into the present century. The earth was Mother Earth indeed and

its composition underfoot the crucial fact in every farmer's life. It is a point that cannot be overstated.

Land varies enormously in fertility and configuration, some tracts being flatter or hillier, the soil lighter or heavier, making them easier or more difficult to work. Such conditions dictate what can be grown and also what could be built. For example a soil that could not grow corn might sustain sheep, but without corn the peasant could not thatch his roof; he had to find a substitute, and one that was near to hand: sod or stone slabs perhaps. Equally if there was no stone on his land he had to build his house with what *was* there, usually clay or wood – though wood became increasingly rare.

Mixed farming in the southwest: sunflowers and hay.

Exactly what was built depended on the soil again. Wheat and grapes for instance call for very different types of storage. In wheat-growing areas, large barns – preferably vermin proof – were needed to protect the harvest and the big stone barns of Champagne and the Beauce are a result. In wine-growing regions however produce had be stored at an even temperature, so cellars were dug or annexes called *chais* built on the north wall of houses. The winepress needed shelter too. Therefore as crops changed in order to accommodate different soils the appearance of local farmsteads followed suit, in layout and materials; forming a taproot in the growth of regional styles.

But to fully understand the farmhouse's very intimate connection with the land we must go briefly underground and start at the very beginning: bedrock. Everything we are to encounter has its origins here, in the three basic categories of rock – for rock is the progenitor of soils as

Topographical map shows France's older and younger mountain ranges – dark and light respectively – her rivers and principal basins.

well as of building stones.

The primal rock is called *igneous* (fiery) rock; it was formed by the initial cooling of the earth's molten minerals. Granite, basalt and lava are of this type and they are found in the oldest mountain ranges and the volcanoes.

The second category of rock is *sedimentary*. Made from the detritus of weathered and eroded igneous and other rocks desposited in the seas, which once covered most of France, sedimentary rock produces some of the most beautiful and workable of building stones: limestone; also sandstone and shale. And when combined with suitable organic material, soils derived from sedimentary rock can be very fertile.

Both igneous and sedimentary rock are changed by heat or pressure into a third category, *metamorphic* rock. In this process limestone becomes marble, and clays and shale are changed into slate and schist.

Such then are the building blocks of France and, when broken down, the inorganic components of French soil – which includes clay, the source of cob and brick.

In France the oldest mountain chains where igneous rock is found are not the familiar ranges of the Alps and Pyrénées but the considerably less salient Armorican Massif in Brittany, the Massif Central that spreads across south-central France, and the low-lying Vosges and Ardennes hills in the northeast. Formed 300 million years ago these mountains have slowly eroded into the stubby plateaux and hills we see today. Their young cousins, the Alps and Pyrénées, one fifth the age of their venerable relations are, being more recent, not only much higher but composed of largely different materials, such as metamorphic schist.

Between these mountainous regions old and young stretch the vast Paris and Aquitaine basins, fertile sedimentary plains in some places further enriched by a thin coat of loess – the residue of ancient glacial erosion. Highly productive they are (respectively) a breadbasket and market garden, but their soil is also rich in clay and in limestone of various hardnesses and hues.

And spreading across all in a great glittering web flow France's myriad rivers, supplying her with two other requisites of agrarian life: a water source and, for centuries, a mode of transportation.

This then *very* briefly is the geologic landscape of France: it is the end product of weathering, upheaval and the breaking down of rock, and it forms the sum and parts of this story. For the houses that stand in it, huddled on hillsides, spread out along the river valleys, or grouped in close-knit villages on the plains, reveal as readily as a geologist's map the composition of the soil beneath them.

LANDHOLDING

In a world where everything came from the land it is easy to see why all men wanted some, and why some wanted a lot. Landholding meant wealth, or at the very least it promised sustenance; but without it there was no security of any kind. So landholding quickly became the basis of the social order and the system that informed it in Europe, feudalism, was by the 10th century already well-established. It is important here because this system survived in France for over 800 years, or until the Revolution in 1789. And many of its traditions continued afterwards, especially patterns of landholding and common pasturing which, despite a revolution, proved very difficult to alter. Houses too continued to reflect the feudal hierarchy, with each social class inhabiting a different type of dwelling (see page 16).

Of France's 30,000 villages, virtually all were in existence by the Middle Ages, forming the central core of every farming community. The villagers had grouped together for water, protection and because fields were communally worked and there was common grazing for their animals. But each village was also a cell in the larger organism of a *seigneurie*. The *seigneurie* comprised a lord's domain (his dwelling, its grounds and a home farm) plus the other territories under his aegis – and this might include several villages and their surrounding fields.

Theoretically seigneurs owned all the land but some peasants became freeholders of a sort, able to sell their land to others, though rarely without its accompanying feudal dues (which were attached to land, not people). Many other peasants were serfs and in the Franche-Comté and parts of Burgundy this practice continued until the Revolution. But between these two extremes there arose the various sorts of tenant farmers who made up the bulk of the peasantry; while at the bottom were the landless – day labourers and semi-nomads who, as population grew, became more numerous.

Usually a *seigneurie* contained some forest or woodland where peasants could gather firewood and graze their pigs; privileges they had to pay for. It also contained meadows and/or heath for grazing – some of it communal land shared by all the villagers. There was a bakehouse and flour mill owned by the lord, which peasants were ordered to use exclusively, one sixth of processed grain being a typical milling fee.

With time however many of these conditions were relaxed and, though seigneurial dues retained the force of law, they became less onerous – mainly because of inflation. They also bought less in return since policing and judicial powers, formerly exercised by lords, were subsumed by an increasingly powerful Crown, that began to levy taxes too. By the 17th century French peasants carried on their backs an unholy trinity of church, crown and nobility and, supporting the lot, they got little or nothing in return.

At this period a new group of landowners made its appearance in the countryside. Victims of inflation, many nobles had to sell off land for ready cash and the buyers were the bourgeoisie who had made money in the towns. It is worth remembering that bourgeois literally means 'of the town'.

Some bourgeois bought *seigneuries* and raised themselves into the aristocracy but others bought land strictly for investment – and expected to reap a good return. They hired agents to see to it, causing much friction among their tenants who saw land as a way of life and not a means of getting rich. Regarded as interlopers and profiteers, bourgeois landowners ignited an animosity between the town and country that became endemic in French society.

Peasants, far the largest sector of the populace, were themselves divided into echelons according to land tenure. On the top rung were the 'big farmers' or *fermiers*, freeholders with enough capital to lease more land and profitably extend their enterprises. This group was mainly in the north, farming the cereal-rich plains of Brie, Picardy and the Beauce, where nearby cities like Lille and Paris provided huge markets for their produce.

Below the big farmers came those freeholders and tenant farmers who possessed enough land to make ends meet so long as things went smoothly. But in any case French farms were small – too small. It has been estimated that five hectares or about twelve acres were needed on average to support a family, yet as late as 1862 only twenty-five per cent of peasant families owned that much; the majority depended on renting extra land or taking outside jobs in order to make ends meet.

A yet lower rung on the landholding ladder was occupied by sharecroppers *(métayers)*. Sharecropping had become attractive to 16th century landowners as a hedge against inflation and in the next two hundred years it spread across the country, becoming particularly widespread in the poorer regions of the west, centre and southwest. In *métayage,* as the sharecropping system was called, the landowner totally provisioned his tenant: land, house, tools and seed. And in return the landlord got half the harvest. Sharecropping leases were often short and even in the 19th century had feudal-sounding clauses demanding regular

Prints of French peasants dated 1564.

deliveries of eggs and vegetables to the landlord's door.

A word must be said about leases in general. In the 16th century leases of between 27 and 59 years were normal but Henri IV (1589-1610) shortened them to six years, and later nine and even three year lets became common. Often leases contained clauses stipulating specific if increasingly archaic farming practices, usually to do with crop rotation and communal grazing; and many leases actively discouraged land development. In Brittany a tenant might own his house but pay a ground rent and he could be thrown off the land at any time, reimbursed as the lord saw fit for the value of his property. Other leases stipulated that property be returned in its original state, thus preventing alterations or even improvements.

Beneath those fortunate enough to keep a toehold on the soil were the day labourers or *brassiers* (arms), the better off of whom were cottagers who might even own their tiny one-roomed dwelling and patch of kitchen garden; but who had no land to farm. Many who were bachelors lived in the house of a master, sleeping in the stable but sharing the family meals and fireside. In 1851, forty-four per cent of men in agriculture were day labourers.

When the Revolution erupted in 1789 three-quarters of France's population were peasants; they owned half the land and cultivated all of it; the remaining half being divided almost equally between church, nobility and bourgeoisie.

But inflation and bourgeois investment had wrought big changes in the existing feudal system and rent, not feudal dues, had become the focus of landlord-tenant agreements. In dismantling the creaking feudal skeleton therefore very little was materially changed: the peasants continued to rent land as before. Moreover estates belonging to the church and *emigré* nobles were auctioned in blocks too large for peasants to buy, so that the beneficiaries were usually the bourgeoisie.

Nevertheless large numbers of peasants managed willy-nilly to increase, if marginally, their tiny holdings and many for the first time bought small plots. By 1882 three-quarters of farms were owner-occupied, yet *farms rented from landlords made up half the cultivated land:* in other words things were not much changed. Moreover new laws of inheritance that divided property equally among offspring made it difficult to hold farms together; but in fact the law was often bent, especially in the patriarchal south where farms as a rule continued to pass to a chosen inheritor.

By encouraging the growth of small family-owned farms the Revolution had fostered a healthy independence but it had also reinforced the age-old pattern of subsistence farming – and with it the *status quo.*

Most farmers worked a tiny plot from which they extracted, with luck and incessant labour, enough to feed their family and pay what rent they owed. Only in the latter half of the 19th century did things begin very slowly to change and it was during this time that most of France's surviving farmhouses were built.

Revolutionary cartoon depicts church and nobility supported on the back of the peasantry.

La Fermiere en Corvé.

THE HOUSING HIERARCHY

CHATEAUX The medieval nobility built castles that, primarily defensive, also advertised their wealth and puissance. Originally wood, stone-built chateaux date from the 10th century. They housed the lord's family and, in times of unrest, his tenants; the battlements, keep, barbican and curtain walls being built to withstand lengthy sieges.

By the late 15th century however military emphasis had given way to a desire for comfort, and power declared itself in ostentatious display: the famous Loire chateaux being the prime examples. Henceforth, *château fort* was used to refer to fortified castles while *châteaux des plaisances* more accurately described the elaborate Renaissance palaces that became the rage.

After the Revolution, 'chateau' described any number of grand country houses, especially if resplendent with towers and set in a landscaped park. In wine-growing areas like Bordeaux the term was further widened to include the seats of prosperous vineyards, with little or no regard for their architecture.

MANORS were originally seigneurial dwellings without sufficient defences to resist a lengthy siege, *i.e.* developed towers and a keep. Nevertheless, many manors were fortified: moats, machicolations and slit windows being by no means rare. Built on a more intimate scale than chateaux, some manors are little more than grandiose farmhouses, often distinguished by a stair turret and two storeys.

Very few extant manors predate the 15th century and, unlike 'chateau', 'manor' was never used to describe post-revolutionary houses.

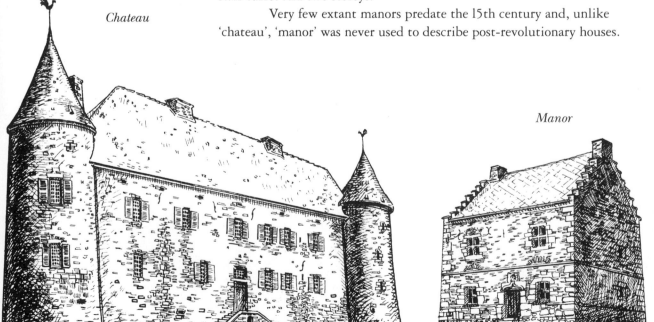

Chateau

Manor

GENTILHOMMIERES Though bourgeois landowners had little direct involvement with farming, many built country houses as summer residences. The style of these houses tended to mimic town fashions rather than local building traditions; nor did *gentilhommières* need the outbuildings necessary to a farm.

A variation of *gentilhommière* is the *chartreuse,* a one-storeyed country house, its central wing normally flanked by pavilions.

MAISON DE MAITRE, or master's house, signified a substantial country dwelling, usually two storeys with an attached farmstead and tenants. Designed for gentlemen who lived off agricultural rents, after the Revolution many *maisons de maître* became the property of active farmers and vintners, and have remained so. Built in the 18th and 19th centuries, the house often faced the court of the farmhouse that depended on it.

PEASANT HOUSES reflected social position principally in their organisation as *farmsteads* since more attention was invariably given to housing livestock and harvest than families. At the top were the big courtyard farms of the northern plains, and some of these establishments are vast – though not their dwellings. The houses of big farmers, small freeholders, tenant farmers and sharecroppers (this last called *métairies*) are generally on a par, their dimensions the result of local traditions and not wealth. These farmsteads form the bulk of peasant housing and are the central focus of this book.

Borderies were sharecropping tenures on the 'borders' of an estate and, as might be expected, the houses were generally very plain, though always in the local style.

LABOURERS and FISHERMEN lived in one-roomed cottages often with a patch of kitchen garden attached. They had no outbuildings.

Gentilhommière

Maison de Maître

Farmhouse

Labourer's Cottage

AGRICULTURE

Sickle

From an early period the French countryside was divided into three agricultural regions whose character depended not on topography or crops but on different field systems that continue today.

'Openfields' refers to the fertile plains of the north: Picardy, Flanders, Champagne, Alsace-Lorraine and the Beauce, where farmland consists of long strips unenclosed by hedges or fencing. Many fields have rounded contours, being at one time segments of a circle surrounding a farming village. The lack of fencing was due to an ancient practice endemic in France of allowing communal grazing on arable land; this meant that after a harvest animals belonging to the whole community roamed at will across the open terrain.

In the west, from Brittany to the Massif Central, the country gives the impression of being everywhere heavily wooded, but when viewed from any hilltop this proves to be an illusion: the landscape is in fact composed of innumerable fields, some of them very small, enclosed by earthen banks one or two metres high and planted with trees. This is the famous French *bocage,* whose name derives from 'wood'. Its proliferation may be due to early cattle raising, particularly in parts of Brittany; but there were agronomic advantages too: in addition to forming windbreaks the trees helped to fix the humidity, creating an improved microclimate in this indifferently fertile region. The *bocage* may also have had a defensive aspect for, as Balzac pointed out, it was almost impossible for an invading army to sweep successfully across its corrugated grid.

Scythe

The south is more complex, a mixture of small fields of irregular shapes – triangles, trapezoids etc – together with regularly laid out rectangles, a legacy from Roman times. And woven into this arable crazy quilt are stretches of low, bracken and brush-covered hills – the *garrigues* of the southeast – once valuable grazing lands and sources of firewood and fodder.

The differences marking these three areas – all of which at one time practised the same agriculture – are mysterious, but evidence points to influences from three separate cultural traditions: Frankish in the north, Celtic in the west, and Roman or Mediterranean in the south. Their housing traditions were equally distinct. The Teutonic Franks built dwellings of clay and wood, a style still popular in Picardy, Champagne and Alsace; while in the Midi, Roman occupation established a tradition of stone masonry that continues to the present day. In the *bocage* stone and clay traditions co-exist, yet their origins appear to be neither Roman nor Frankish: the technique of dry-stone construction (building without mortar) dates back to the prehistoric era of menhirs and dolmens, found throughout the region, while clay and wattle owes much to Viking settlements, especially in Normandy.

Subsistence farming was the rule in all three regions. This meant each family produced everything it needed; nothing was bought and very little sold. The drawback to this often idyllic-sounding life will soon be seen but its pattern went something like this: on arable land a farmer grew corn for bread; he had a patch of hemp or flax for making cloth; a small orchard *(verger)* provided seasonal fruit and a vegetable garden *(potager)* next to the house supplied soup greens. He might also keep a cow, some chickens, a pig and, depending on the region, a few sheep probably reared on common land. But the staple crop was always corn *(le blé)*. It has been said that French peasants were obsessed with corn but they had to be, since famine was a regular visitor. A wet harvest, a hailstorm or an early frost could destroy all foodstuff for the coming year; and a peasant who lost his harvest had no means of replacing it. In the 17th century there were reportedly eleven nationwide famines in France; and in the 18th century sixteen, during which the population could fall by as much as twenty per cent. On top of this, local food crises were rife. It is simply not possible today to comprehend the razor edge of rural life before insurance companies and national welfare agencies – or indeed more efficient production methods – were introduced; though recent famines in Ethiopia and Somalia give some idea.

To most farmers, corn meant rye, a cereal that did well in indifferent soil. Wheat, largely confined to better soils and home-farms of the nobility, fed the rich with white bread. Peasant bread was black. But even rye could not be grown everywhere and in very poor areas, parts of Limousin, Dordogne and the Cévennes for instance, chestnuts were consumed instead of bread.

The tools that were used to till the land were the same in the 19th century as in 12th: spade, plough, pitchfork, axe, harrow, hoe, rake, sickle, pruning hook and flail. Scythes were rarely used: able to cut three times faster than a sickle, it was felt they cut the corn too low and did not leave either sufficient straw for fodder or enough grain for gleaners to gather after the harvest.

In the north a heavy wheeled plough *(charrue)* pulled by horses proved more efficient than the light swing plough *(araire)* traditional in the south, where ploughing continued to be done with oxen.

Harrow

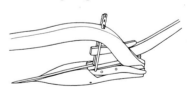

Southern plough: araire

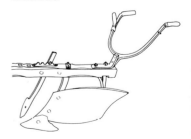

Northern plough: charrue

Another practice different in north and south was crop rotation. Both areas practised fallowing to prevent exhaustion of the soil, but in the north a three-field system prevailed, and in the south, two-field. This meant that one third and one half (respectively) of arable land lay fallow at any time, a fact that horrified the Englishman Arthur Young, touring the country shortly before the Revolution. Fallowing had long since disappeared in England, as indeed had famines; but France was locked in a vicious agrarian circle which, despite repeated and fearful food shortages, she was unable to break; and two factors were largely responsible – communal pasturing on arable, mentioned above, and an acute shortage of fertilizer.

Communal grazing meant the harvest must begin and end on a stated day so that the animals could be let loose. This custom prevented the enclosure of fields, and therefore the initiation of new and experimental techniques. Although the Revolution, in supporting individual rights, endorsed enclosures, local resistance was fierce and the practice of communal pasturing *(vaine pâture)* was not formally abolished in France till 1899.

The problem of fertilizer was even more basic. A cow ate 10kg of hay each day which meant few families could rear more than one. This in turn meant there was very little manure for the fields so yields could not be increased and therefore more livestock could not be reared. There seemed to be no way out. Cereal yields in the early 19th century were the same as in 1500: on average five grains reaped for each one sown. Today the norm in France is 20 to 1 and fertilizers are largely responsible.

Chemical fertilizers were introduced into France in the 19th century. Expensive and slow to catch on, they nevertheless enabled new meadowland known as artifical prairies to be planted in forage crops (chiefly lucerne). The results were spectacular. Far richer than natural meadows, livestock could now be reared in significantly greater numbers, and so more fertilizer became available. The old cycle continued for a while but circumstances, now much improved, admitted leeway. And for the first time there were surpluses.

More improvements were to follow. Crop rotation without fallowing, practised in next-door Flanders for three hundred years, slowly began to be adopted, first on the northern plains then gradually spreading throughout the south and central regions. The secret of no-fallow rotation was to alternate short-rooted cereal crops with long-rooted legumes, *e.g.* beet, potatoes and turnips that fed deeper in the soil: in other words, growing on two levels. This meant the amount of land under cultivation at any one time virtually doubled. Suddenly famine became a thing of the

Opposite: J-F Millet's famous picture The Angelus revealed but helped to romanticise peasant life.

past and there were sufficient surpluses to be marketed.

The agricultural revolution of the mid-19th century had far greater impact on peasant life than the political revolution a century earlier. In addition to fertilizers and intensive crop rotation an improved plough meant previously uncultivable land could now be exploited. New crops from America – maize, potatoes and beans – became widely established, maize having already replaced rye as the staple crop feeding man and beast in Aquitaine.

With the fear of bread shortages removed, specialization was increasingly attractive; but it was railways that made the move to a market economy really feasible: cash crops and surpluses could now be shipped rapidly and efficiently all over the country.

The old pattern of subsistence farming was on the wane: in Normandy a prosperous dairy industry developed and milk, butter and cheeses were sent daily to the Paris markets. On the northern plains, the patchwork of subsistence crops was transformed into the intensively cultivated wheat and sugarbeet cultures that we see today. Viticulture, the only specialized crop heretofore, began to blanket the hills of Languedoc after the disease phylloxera wiped out the country's vineyards, many of which were never replanted. Market gardens sprouted in the Garonne river valley and large-scale sheep farming enriched the remote Gévaudan and arid Rouergue *causses.* In the Cévennes hills a flourishing silkworm industry began.

Changes in agriculture necessitated changes in farm buildings, as will be shown. Dairies, sheepfolds, piggeries, prune ovens and *magnaneries* for silkworms are examples. France's rural world had taken a step forward, its first of any note since the Middle Ages.

The Second Empire (1852 to 1870) were golden years in the French countryside: the old traditions, though improved, remained in place and prosperity could everywhere be seen. It was during this time that the

Oxen, still in use in the Pyrénées Ariège.

idealised peasant world depicted in innumerable prints and paintings became widespread. On walls throughout France, and indeed all over Europe, muscular well-fed farmers heaved hay on to burgeoning wagons and wizened faces round a cottage fire listened rapturously to thrice-told tales. Most popular of all, Millet's gentle peasants, their heads bowed in humble thanksgiving, stood in a cornfield during the angelus. The idyll of peasant life had seized the public's imagination.

But what was it all about? Peasant life had been a reviled and piteous state, and those migrating to the towns had willingly left behind their repetitive and backbreaking toil. Part of the answer may be that, in order to become bearable, terrible hardships often receive a subsequent gloss; it is the seed of epic poetry and many a heroic tale. But another factor also played a part: romanticism. Man's oldest and perhaps most cherished dream has been to live at peace in the bosom of his traditional enemy Nature; a return to paradise indeed, but one that was only achievable through Nature's subjugation. Suddenly, it had become a possibility.

The next step forward is merely a postscript in this story; it did not occur until the 1950s and broke forever the centuries-old mould of the past. In 1929 there were some 30,000 tractors in France, mainly on the northern plains. Thirty years later the figure had reached a million and for the first time France was producing more than she could use. Farming could become a business, with agricultural exports earning foreign exchange.

In this sort of climate however smallholdings ceased to make sense: farms had to be bigger to compete and to sustain investment in new and expensive equipment. Between 1955 and 1988 the number of farms was halved and the average farm size doubled. The massive exodus to towns meant whole villages were deserted and dwellings that had sheltered generations of peasants crumbled into ruins. But farm yields continued to rise: in 1960, 25 quintals of wheat per hectare was produced in the Paris basin and by 1990 even this figure had been tripled. After centuries of repeated food shortages, France was suffering from an embarrassment of riches. By 1981 she was the world's largest exporter of food after the United States. But in order to make over-production viable crops had to be heavily subsidized; other countries were overproducing too.

The situation could not last and today, as farm subsidies are being reduced or removed, French agriculture is once again poised on a razor's edge. Surpluses have become as threatening to the preservation of modern rural life as shortages were for so many centuries in the past. It appears that Nature's subjugation, although substantially achieved, has not so far brought paradise – at least not for those who till the soil.

HABITAT

A farmhouse was, then, considerably more than just a family dwelling. Sheltering livestock, harvest and farm equipment, often under one roof, it functioned as an agricultural tool and no farmer would have dreamt of considering his livestock or crops as separate from or less important than the family, or his barn as less important than his house. The concepts of farmhouse and farmstead were indistinguishable. The outsider who buys a French farmhouse often fails to see this connection and thinks nothing of dismantling an old bake oven or piggery – as much a part of the house when it was built as was its chimney.

Rather like ships, farmsteads were self-contained units that had to be stocked with all the requisites needed to survive a land voyage easily as risky as the sea. Good luck was essential and to that end various rituals accompanied a house's construction. In Brittany coins were placed under the cornerstone and the blood of a cock sprinkled over the foundations; otherwise the first person to enter the house would die within the year. Wall timbers in Alsace formed arcane good luck patterns – becoming part of the local style – and, in efforts to ward off evil, runic symbols, usually geometric in shape, were set into brick work, painted on walls and cut into posts and shutters in regions as far afield as Alsace, Flanders and the Basque country. When the house was finished a plant was usually set on the rooftop, the house was then blessed by a priest and prayers were said for its protection and that of the occupants. It was rather like launching a ship.

A number of houses also had symbolic roles, as emblems of family entity and perpetuity. This was especially true of patriarchal households in the south and east where several generations often shared one roof. In the Basque country for example the house name became the family surname and certain civic roles were tied to property and inherited or sold with it.

Opposite: stone-flagged veranda in the Tarare mountains shows the unselfconscious clutter of a working farm.

THE BASIC TYPES

A traveller in the countryside will tell you there are as many types of farmhouses as localities and it is true that there are many regional styles, each with individual offspring as will be shown; but despite this rich diversity of forms, every French farmhouse falls into one of four categories, each one a different approach to lodging a family *and* its agricultural belongings safely and efficiently.

The Basic House

The basic house or *maison bloc* is at its simplest the oldest housing plan in existence, and it remains the dominant farmhouse style in France. In *maisons blocs* man and animals lodged side by side under one roof, enabling both livestock and family to be protected at close range and the animals to be more easily cared for. Food and fodder stored in the house's loft completed this self-contained and compact unit.

Originally family and livestock had shared one room, gradually separating to opposite ends of what became known as a longhouse (fig 1); the family at one end, their livestock at the other. A waist-high partition and finally a wall arose dividing the two domains which, at their most evolved, have separate entrances. Longhouse development can best be seen in Brittany where early, unpartitioned examples still exist, inhabited in this century.

Suited to subsistence farming, *maisons blocs* are found throughout France and several variations of the longhouse have evolved. Quite often for instance the stable is distanced from the dwelling by being at the far end of an attached barn (fig 2), a threshing floor or carthouse in between. But in middle Garonne the dwelling is often in the *middle* of the building, and livestock and storage in the ends (fig 3).

Non-longhouse versions of the *maison bloc* are squarish in shape and many have the stable at the rear (fig 4). Alpine chalets are generally *maisons blocs*. In parts of Guyenne and the Landes however dwelling, carthouse and stable run the length instead of the width of the building, with all the doorways in the gable (fig 5).

1. Early longhouse with central hearth and shared entrance.

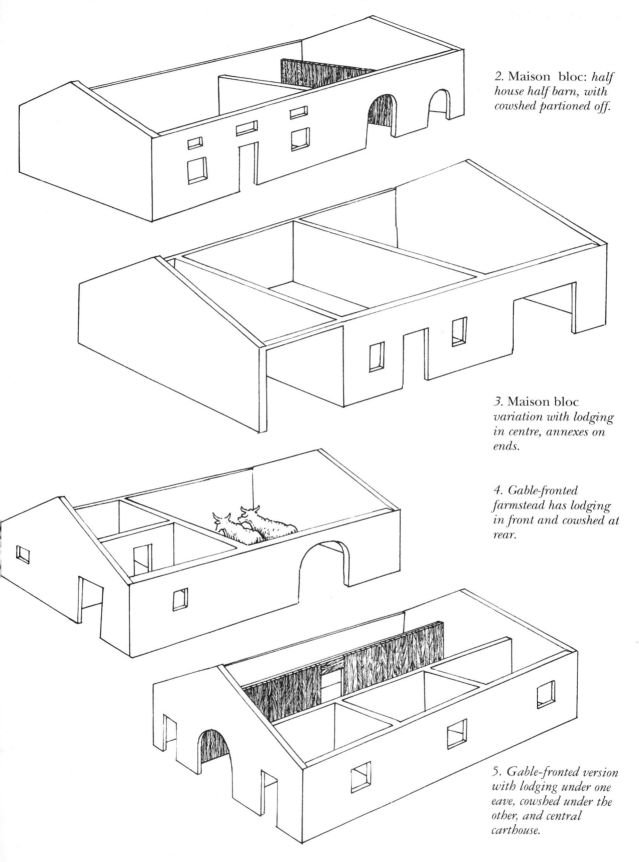

2. Maison bloc: *half house half barn, with cowshed partioned off.*

3. Maison bloc *variation with lodging in centre, annexes on ends.*

4. *Gable-fronted farmstead has lodging in front and cowshed at rear.*

5. *Gable-fronted version with lodging under one eave, cowshed under the other, and central carthouse.*

27

High-House

The high-house *(maison en hauteur)* is distinguished by having the living quarters upstairs and storage or stabling on the floor below. Of Mediterranean origin, it was normally built of stone and its locale in France is mainly the southeast.

A first floor lodging had several advantages: it was more secure in unsettled times than ground floor dwellings and in winter the presence of cattle below and hay in the loft produced a well-insulated central heating system.

High-houses had the additional convenience of being superior wine stores: the ground floor temperature is fairly constant and large wine barrels could easily be stored without hoisting. This explains the spread of high-houses into the wine-growing regions of Burgundy and the Mâconnais, and their ubiquity in Provence, Languedoc and what were once wine-growing areas like the Auvergne. But in mountainous regions – the Ariège, Basque country, the Cévennes and parts of the Alps – the ground floor continued to belong to livestock.

Ground floors had another use too, as spinning and weaving workrooms. Linen fibres had to be kept humid or the thread would break and high-houses provided the right conditions. This accounts for their unexpected appearance in Brittany, around Léon, where an active linen trade flourished in the 18th century.

Most high-houses have an exterior stone stair leading to a terrace which is either open or covered by an awning or projection of the roof. In Béarn and some alpine chalets however entry is by an interior stair located in the 'barn'.

Opposite: flower bedecked high-house in the Beaujolais is stylistically very different from the Quercy-style below (note pisé-built upper storey).

High-house stairs run parallel or perpendicular to the facade, and most are covered.

Courtyard Farmstead

The courtyard farmstead *(maison cour)* has, as its name suggests, lodging and outbuildings disposed around a court. A wall often completed the enclosure and many big farmsteads boast an imposing gateway. Courtyard farmsteads are associated with wealth and one of their antecedents was the Roman villa, a self-contained walled quadrangle opening on to an inner court. The large farmsteads of the Paris basin, Picardy and Languedoc strongly reflect this antique influence.

The courtyard style is essentially a defensive arrangement but, as special housing for different animals developed – chicken houses, piggeries, etc – it was more useful to bend them round a court than keep on adding to a house's length.

Farmsteads can be 'open' in plan as well as 'closed' – the buildings need not be joined, but it has been suggested that the increase in closed court farmsteads in the north might be due to the use of horses instead of oxen for ploughing (horses have to be corralled).

The arrangement of buildings round the court varied according to the region: in Alsace and Béarn for example the house is at right angles to the entrance; in Normandy it is opposite. But whatever the arrangement, the farmer could always survey from his window activities in the court outside. In a few a dovecote rose impressively but without exception they contained a mountainous dunghill *(fumier)* steadily accumulating highly valued manure.

Scattered Dwelling

The scattered dwelling *(maison en ordre lâche).* In this type of farmstead outbuildings are dispersed haphazardly in relation to the house. The chief examples are upper Normandy and the Landes where outbuildings are scattered about the farmstead in no particular plan. In the former it made sense to keep valuable stores away from thatched dwellings with their volatile chimneys, while in the pine plantations of the Landes there was the continual danger of forest fires and among other outbuildings freestanding bread ovens helped reduce fire hazard.

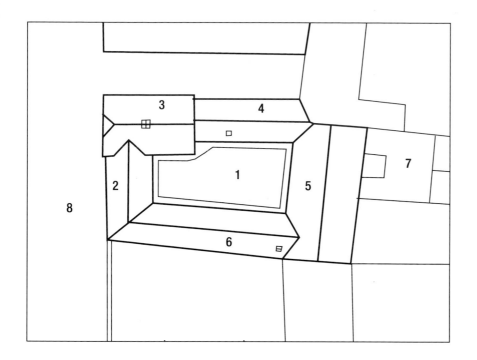

1. court
2. covered porch
3. house
4. annexes
5. barn
6. stable
7. orchard
8. street

Alsation courtyard farmstead. The enclosed court gives on to village street via a porch. The house's gable always faces the street.

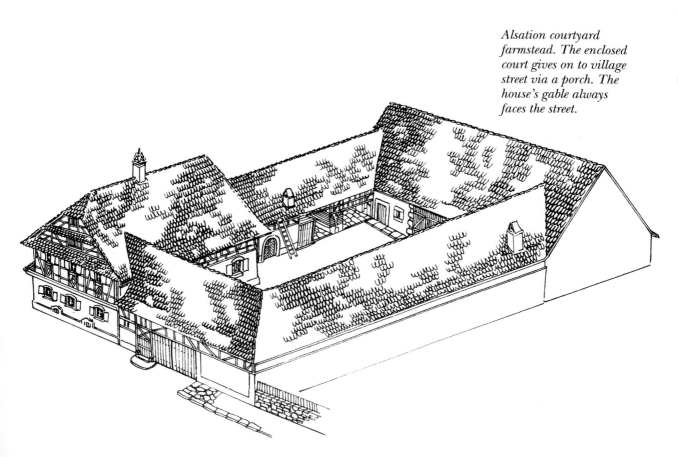

SITING

Most farmhouses face south or southeast, getting the maximum winter sun and keeping their backs against the hostile north. But some houses, especially those near the Atlantic coast, face east away from the prevailing wind. All are virtually blind at the back, *i.e.* without windows or doors, and in parts of central and western France a double rear wall gives many houses additional protection, while hipped roofs help the wind over the house.

The siting of farmsteads *vis à vis* the community depended on several factors. Where there was an abundant water supply houses could disperse, each with its own well; but the problem of security largely prevented this before the 18th century. Villages were safer and many of the oldest, especially those in Provence, were built on hilltops so as to see and ward off enemies. On the plains of northern France however they were usually located at the centre of communal fields. A river, once the chief means of haulage, or a road or crossroads also made convenient focal points – and many villages were walled.

Though the north was much more given to village habitats, the south has many more of them. This is because the south's indifferent soil made smallholdings much more numerous. The south's extended family structure also contributed to the growth of hamlets: second and third generations often building next to their elders in order to share the family land and tools.

But whether farms were isolated or in a village they were part of a *pays* (the word cannot be adequately translated). A *pays* was generally about the distance a man could travel in a day and return home – roughly 20 miles; and within this area lay his entire world: his home, farmland, village, local market town – and probably all his relations, for many peasants never travelled beyond the boundaries of their own *pays*. As a result the *pays* engendered a feeling of belonging and loyalty that amounted to a concentrated form of nationalism.

France comprised a patchwork of these tiny self-regarding entities, each one stitched into the larger pattern of a province and, from a bird's eye view perhaps, a nation. In understanding the lack of change in the countryside, and the existence of so many vernacular styles, the *pays* is a highly important factor.

DATING HOUSES

Dating farmhouses is extremely difficult. Unlike more important buildings vernacular styles rarely reflected contemporary fashion, which could take centuries to find its way into regional peasant traditions (the majority only did so in the 19th century). But keeping in mind that most houses, despite their antique appearances, are mid- to late 19th century, many older houses do have recognizable features.

Unusually thick stone walls a metre or more in width and built *à fruit* (the exterior wall inclining inwards slightly) indicates an older building. So do very small windows and few of them; and really big timbers.

A stone house which also has a timber frame is probably not *later* than the 18th century, while mullioned windows or a stone window seat are earlier, probably 16th or 17th century. Exterior tower stairs are also a sign of great age, being almost exclusively a feature of 15th century manor houses.

But none of the above is foolproof. Moreover materials were routinely re-used. Stones from earlier houses or from Roman and Celtic ruins were regularly incorporated into the walls of farmhouses, while timber-framed houses could be – and often were – pulled down and reassembled in new locations.

Nor are the features mentioned useful as a guide to period construction. Generally speaking, extant peasant houses predating the mid-18th century were more important ones, and therefore better built. They have also been very lucky.

The Renaissance-style doorway in this unoccupied Breton house probably dates from the late 18th century.

MATERIALS & CONSTRUCTION

In the 18th and 19th centuries, country craftsmen were often small farmers, earning money haphazardly in construction; yet it is to them we almost certainly owe the development of regional architectural styles. Working sporadically in towns or nearby chateaux, they learned, if not new skills, new *styles* of building, aimed at enlarging human comfort and ostentation. And some of these they introduced in simplified forms at home. For though slow to transgress time-honoured habits, peasants were none the less mesmerised by doings of the nobility and towns; and glass windows, terracotta tiles, dormers, slate roofs and symmetrical floor plans were among the innovations gradually incorporated into local houses, the builders making their own adjustments as need and inclination arose. And these in turn were copied by the community. An Ile de France dormer therefore is not like one in Périgord.

Two other factors also helped the entrenchment of a local style. In an illiterate society, it made sense to fix the price and style of new houses by using nearby ones as models. Secondly, the peasants themselves were often builders: DIY was part of life and a man and his neighbours, most of whom had assisted in similar tasks, could erect a house or barn with little or no professional help, simply by following constructions in the neighbourhood. If a mason or carpenter was present, however, the family and its neighbours formed his main work force.

None of these circumstances fostered change.

Wood, earth, stone, vegetable matter, and sometimes animal products, were the materials used for building. What was used depended on what was to hand; how it was used, on the range and quality of available skills, and the grain of established traditions. But though materials and building styles varied between locales, building techniques did not: roughly the same everywhere, they hardly changed in France from the end of the Middle Ages to this century.

Houses are largely built in times of abundance and/or growing population and in France these were the early 17th century (following the Wars of Religion); sporadically in the 18th century, as population grew, and large-scale during the 19th century agricultural boom (Second Empire). Despite their deceptively antique appearances, however, few farmhouses standing today predate the 18th century and the majority were built in the mid- to late 19th century – though some incorporate older

parts and materials. Fewer than one in a thousand 17th century houses are believed to have survived. Famine, wars and political unrest were largely to blame, but the insubstantial nature of much early housing also played a part.

Before the 15th century, peasant houses were often improvised constructions of branches covered with sod or brush, while the more refined were of wattle and daub. Of whatever material however houses tended to be round or oval shaped, since corners were difficult to construct. Nor was there a proper chimney. A hole in the roof emitted smoke or it went out through the door. (Houses of this sort were occupied in Brittany and the Landes in this century.)

The tradition of stone work, continuous in the southeast, spread with the 12th century growth of chateaux and monasteries. But stone was not much used among the peasantry before the 16th century, when gable chimneys also begun to be built. Gradually, however, it displaced wattle and daub wherever usable stone was on hand.

Though chateaux and town styles continued to influence the peasantry, progress was extremely slow and a 15th century stone farmhouse excavated in Burgundy was not greatly different from dwellings built 400 years later – tiled flooring, a gable chimney and windows being the main improvements. In size, layout and building materials they were the same. For though building materials continued to come from the earth, the expense of transforming them – turning clay into bricks or burning lime for mortar – was too costly for most people before the 19th century. In using products of the soil, however, builders had tapped a very considerable store – of which three materials had prime importance: oak, limestone and clay.

MATERIALS

WOOD was essential to construction and a house's width often depended on the length of timbers available to span its walls. Oak was preferred for all the major timbers, then chestnut; while poplar and elm supplied the material for doors, window frames and shutters. In mountainous regions, larch and spruce were split into shingles while pine supplied secondary timbers in softwood areas like the Landes.

Most often trees were cut in winter or late autumn and soaked in water to remove the tannin. Then the timber was dried and, if clients could wait, aged for about a year. Proper seasoning hardens wood, making it more resistant to insects and fungus.

Oak, because of its rock-like hardness when seasoned – as anyone who has put a fingernail into an old oak beam will know – was cut to required lengths while the wood was green, its radial veins providing a natural cleaving pattern. In older houses the beams were squared with an adze. (Oak is highly resistant to woodworm, a constant hazard in France, and infested wood needs treatment chiefly to prevent its spread to other woods nearby.)

By medieval times, large timbers were already a rarity. Abbot Suger's carpenters doubted that 12 oaks of sufficient size could be found to complete his new basilica of St Denis, and scarcity may have had a part in the switch from wood to stone for building after the 16th century. In any event, large timbers would rarely have been at the disposal of peasants. Forests were private preserves and though peasants might gather wood and graze their cattle there, they were not empowered to fell trees. Even on common land such rights were usually prohibited: a royal edict issued by Louis XIV reserved all large timbers for building ships. But some farmers grew their own timber, planting banks that enclosed their fields with oaks and beeches. Felled as needed they could also be coppiced regularly for repairs to house and barns. This practice helped create the *bocage* landscape in western France.

STONE Granite, limestone, schist, sandstone and flint offered masons a palette of greys, pink, chocolate, fawn and pure white, each with its own special texture. The stones were either rubble 'freestones' gathered in nearby fields, or were quarried locally – the latter option becoming feasible with improved transport in the 19th century. It has been estimated that in the Middle Ages transporting stone for 10 miles doubled its cost, and there is little reason to see why this would have changed.

Limestone *(pierre calcaire)* was the most desirable stone for building, some of the best coming from around Caen, also Charente-Périgord and the Soissonnais.

Most limestone walling was rubble stone *(moellons),* used as found or hewn into quasi-rectangular blocks that could be laid in courses. Dressed stone *(pierre de taille)* was reserved for quoins and to frame windows and doors. It helped to strengthen rubble walls and protect corners from damage, contrasting pleasantly with the different texture of the walls. Dressed stone walls were rare in the countryside except in areas like the Gironde where stone was soft enough to be easily cut — and the wine trade sufficiently prosperous to pay for it.

Tufa *(tuffeau),* a soft, pumice-like limestone, was readily cut into blocks, which made it easier to lay. The most beautiful came from Touraine where it was seasoned before use, sometimes for many years, in order to harden it. But later on the practice fell into disuse causing subsequent problems. Alternatively, tufa was rendered to protect its crumbly surface from erosion.

Chalk *(craie)* is another form of crumbly limestone. The best quality was cut into handsome marble-like blocks and often combined with brick to make an attractive pattern as in Champagne and Flanders.

Schist *(schiste)* is, like limestone, a naturally layered rock. Quarried in flat plaques, it stacks with comparative ease, but corners were difficult to construct and again dressed stone was needed for quoins and window frames. Some schist walls were mounted dry, an ancient practice using skills that have virtually disappeared in France. Schist was also used for roofing tiles.

Granite *(granit)* built houses are common in Brittany, Morvan and the Massif Central; but few predate the 18th century. This is probably due to the difficulties of working this intransigent stone with the available tools. Coloured pink in some areas, a brooding grey is characteristic. But granite's somewhat depressing austerity is balanced by the awesome size of many of the stones: in Brittany, for example, huge monolithic boulders frame windows and doors with spectacular effect.

Basalt *(basalte),* a black volcanic stone almost as hard as granite was much used in parts of the Auvergne.

Flint *(silex),* being impervious to humidity, provided a first class material (where available) for foundations. It was also used as walling in combination with materials like adobe and limestone, alternated in attractive chequerboard or banded patterns. Flint is plentiful in Picardy, upper Normandy and Champagne.

Sandstone *(grès)* varies in quality and colour: some of the most beautiful, called Roussard stone, is found in Mayenne, while that in western Corrèze has made the wine-red village of Collonges-la-Rouge famous throughout France.

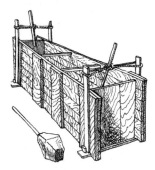

1. Torchis applied to a trellis work.

2. Mould for compressing pisé *clay mixture for walling.*

3. Sun-dried adobe brick mould.

4. Burned brick was used for surrounds.

EARTH, or more precisely, mud, is an excellent material for building. Freely available and requiring little skill to work, its isothermic qualities are first-class: a mud house stays cool in summer and warm in winter, and is also remarkably soundproof. Properly built and protected from water, earthen walls will stand for generations. 'All mud needs is a hat and a good pair of shoes,' the old saying goes, and some of France's finest civil architecture is made of it.

The essential ingredient in mud construction is clay, the product of ancient rock breakdown of all kinds, including granite. Obtained by digging below the topsoil, clay's adhesive qualities are admirably suited for construction. But because it shrinks and therefore cracks as it dries, a lot of sand must be added. Silt, inert matter normally already present in clay soil, is needed too.

Three raw earth mixtures have dominated French construction: *pisé* and *torchis* (forms of cob), and adobe. A fourth, *bauge,* is rarer. All involve mixing clay, silt, sand and water but consistency varies; more importantly, each was used in a different manner to construct a wall.

Traditionally clay was dug in early autumn so that winter weathering would make it ready for use by the spring. It was then mixed in the hole where it had been dug, by trampling with bare feet. In areas like the Grande Brière in Brittany, the process took on a festive quality as the men linked arms dancing and singing in the mud. Afterwards, the hole became a pond for livestock and barnyard fowls.

Torchis, the most renowned of raw earth methods, was used to infill timber-framed buildings. A form of wattle and daub, the *torchis* mixture was applied to a trellis work erected between the framing timbers (fig l). (The process is described under Walling). A comparatively plastic mix, *torchis* also contains straw pieces 6 or 8 inches long, preferably beginning to rot. Sometimes animal hair or lime was added and sometimes dung, the latter variant known as *bouseli.*

Pisé is a stiffer mixture than *torchis* and it contains gravel. It was used in a process called *banchage* in which the *pisé* was forked into a large 'mould' made of shutters (fig 2). Again, the process is described under Walling.

Adobe *(brique crue).* The technique of making sun-dried bricks is thought to have entered Europe from North Africa via Spain. As with *torchis,* a little chopped straw, hay or fibrous litter was added to wet clay which was then mixed with a hoe or trampled with the feet. The wet mixture was packed into a four-sided wooden mould (fig 3) and smoothed with a wire bow. Then the mould was removed and the adobe sun-dried for two or three days, first flat and then on edge. Careful drying was necessary to prevent deformation. In a second drying, bricks were stacked in open-work piles for about a month.

The size of French adobe moulds varied, two of the most popular being 'toulousain' measuring 25x35x5cm and 'auvergne', the same thickness, but smaller: 12x20cm.

Bauge is a mixture somewhere between *torchis* and *pisé* in which earth, sand and straw were kneaded into lumps or large balls and hand-packed in layers on to a low foundation. The results are best seen in cottages in the Vendée called *bourrines,* and in the Camargue.

Brick is of course a more sophisticated form of adobe. It was introduced into France by the Romans whose superior cements enabled them to achieve outstanding architectural feats with brick: the famous aquaduct at Nîmes is an example. But after the Roman occupation ended, brickmaking disappeared throughout Europe until the Middle Ages. Re-developed mainly in Holland and Flanders, early brickwork can be seen in southern France around Toulouse, but brick was never a major building material in France till after 1860, flourishing instead as trim (fig 4) or, later on, infill in timber-framed buildings (fig 5).

Like adobe, brick was made in wooden moulds and left in the sun to dry; then it was stacked in a shed for three to six weeks. Originally the brick was fired in small woodburning kilns, as Roman brick had been, but this was an expensive process and fuel consumption is estimated to have equalled 20% of the weight of the final product.

By the early 19th century 'county kilns' appeared in northern France based on Flemish design. Bricks could now be cooked on a vast scale. Combustible material was packed around the bricks – some kilns holding up to 3 million – and burning took two to three weeks.

Though brick sizes have changed over the centuries, the ratio of length to width remains the same: length being double the width plus the width of the join. This allows the brick to be laid in evenly lapping rows or bonds (fig 6). Old brick was broad and flat: only about 3cm thick and up to 35cm long, rather like large terracotta tiles. Modern, machine-made brick (11 x 22 x 5cm) lacks both textural variation and the wonderful patina that results from age. It is however better able to accommodate bricklayers, who can hold a brick in one hand, leaving the other free to work the trowel.

VEGETABLE MATTER was chiefly used as roofing. Corn, reed, bracken, gorse, sedge, bulrushes, furze and turf were all employed; but rye, the staple peasant cereal, was the most common. Rye straw was readily available on most farms; where it was not, broom or bracken served instead. Broom and bracken were also used to clad the walls of sheepfolds and other buildings exposed to rough weather. But the best thatch roof of all was water reed: obtainable along the coastal marshlands, a good water reed roof lasted 60 or 70 years.

5. Brick infill.

6. Classic brick bonds: running (a), English (b), Flemish (c).

MORTARS AND PLASTERS

Rendering exterior walls is customary all over France. It originated as a means of protecting building materials and improving their watertightness – and it became fashionable. But today the fashion is shifting. Where the stone is of good quality, it is often left exposed. Improved mortars have made this practice feasible. But all too often the wrong mortar is used or the joints are over-emphasised, obscuring the natural beauty of the stone.

Because mortars and plasters play such an important role in restoration, it is worth examining the subject in some detail: much confusion exists in both practices and terminology.

In the old days, mortars and plasters (renders) were the same stuff, differently applied; they fell into two categories depending on whether or not they contained lime.

Earth mortar *(mortier de terre)* is a mixture of roughly three parts sand to one part clay. Used in construction everywhere, in the 18th and 19th centuries it began to be phased out as lime became less expensive. But in poorer areas, Brittany for instance, earth mortar continued in use till after World War I; and today all over France houses and barns are held together by it, usually under a good coat of lime plaster.

Slaked lime *(chaux grasse)* is made by breaking down pieces of limestone in a kiln. The cooked pieces – quicklime or *chaux vive* – are then 'slaked' (soaked in water) and combined with sand. The method is explained in the Appendix. Slaked lime is superior to ordinary mud plaster in that it produces a harder more durable finish; but it too is susceptible to water. Dried by air, slaked lime sets very slowly and walls can take many years to develop their full strength. Nevertheless its improved quality enabled higher walls to be built, and so second storeys. Both interiors and exteriors were plastered with it. (It is now possible to buy factory-slaked lime. See Appendix.)

Hydraulic lime *(chaux hydraulique)* is harder still and will set under water. It is made by heating *claybearing* limestone (which contains up to 15% clay). Hydraulic lime is not suitable for restoring old buildings, though many make the mistake of using it, with the result that walls take on an unnatural colouring and cannot breathe.

Both *chaux grasse* and *mortier de terre* have delicate and subtle hues, which vary from region to region: creams, greys, buffs, ochres and browns that blend with the surrounding landscape. This happens because the plaster takes its colour from the local sand with which it is mixed. Hydraulic lime, whose colour is a dismal, battleship grey, does not do this. (A white variety *(chaux blanche)* can be tinted artificially but the results are not particularly successful.)

Plaster of Paris, named because of the gypsum-rich region surrounding the French capital, was used in Ile de France, Burgundy and Provence both as a mortar and for rendering, as well as for plastering interior walls.

Two kinds of plaster were produced: *'au panier'* and *'au sas'*, the former for use outside. Both were obtained by cooking gypsum at a temperature only a fraction of that required for lime, making plaster more economical to use. But in the 1920s the old ovens were abandoned for a different system and the making of exterior-quality plaster ceased: its impurities had made *'au panier'* possible. Today a bastard mortar (see Appendix) can be substituted for repairs.

Limewash *(lait de chaux)* was applied over earthen or lime plaster as further protection against insects and fungus, and to maintain a tidy appearance. Though white predominates, limewash can also be tinted in beautiful earthen tones – some of the most pleasing are seen in Provence. The wash was renewed yearly using a rag or brush attached to a long stick.

1. Shallow foundations were normal practice.

FOUNDATIONS

The foundations of most French farmhouses are, by modern standards, inadequate – if they exist at all. And yet the buildings stand, at worst a prey to rising damp and efflorescences like saltpetre. Even where cellars exist they were generally dug as a separate pit inside the walls of the house.

Natural outcrops of rock were, where possible, integrated into walls as foundations, but more often a shallow trench was dug a few inches to a foot deep and slightly wider than the walls (fig 1). The inside of the trench was levelled and filled with smallish stones so that water could flow through without becoming trapped. Sometimes compacted clay was used as a base instead of stones, but many old houses rest humbly on the soil, their only protection a thin bed of pebbles.

Quite a different solution was to build the foundations above ground. A low wall *(soubassement)* between 50cm and a metre high was erected, the top edge sloping slightly outwards to throw off the water (fig 2). Limestone was the most popular material for *soubassements* but flint and granite, where available, provided better resistance to rising damp. Brick was also used but its high porosity was a drawback and, in Flanders and Picardy, brick foundations were tarred to improve their water resistance. Where earthen walling was used, a raised foundation was essential to protect the walls from damp.

In timber-framed constructions, corner posts were set on stone footings to prevent them from rotting (fig 3).

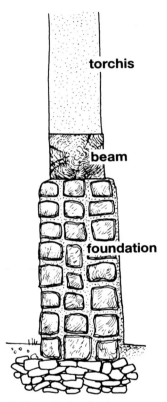

torchis

beam

foundation

2. Foundation built above ground.

3. Stone footing.

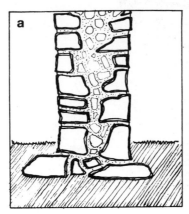

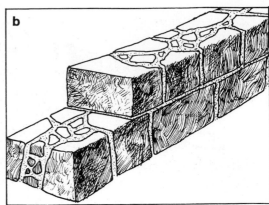

1. Sandwich construction of masonry walls (a) in which transversely-laid stones (b) added strength.

MASONRY WALLS

The vast majority of walls were made of limestone rubble *(moellons)*, sometimes roughly shaped into rectangles, as already described. Limestone walls were constructed like a sandwich, the outer and inner facings filled with a core of smaller stones and mortar (fig 1a). One course was laid at a time: facings first, then the filling, the laying procedure being very roughly two stones over one and one over two. In order to steady the wall, some stones were laid *'en boutisse',* that is, transversely across the sandwich (fig 1b), and occasionally they protruded beyond the walls (fig 2). But the reason for this, though much speculated on, remains a mystery.

Wall thickness varied from 50cm to a metre or more in very old houses, many of which were built *'à fruit'* – the outer face leaning slightly inwards while the inner face remained vertical (fig 3). Accomplished by making the lower wall thicker, this purportedly increased a dwelling's stability.

Because mortar is vulnerable to water it was important to keep the tops of walls well-protected during and after building or the two faces would soon part company. Examples can be seen today in tumbledown houses all over France.

Many walls, schist in particular, needed dressed stones as quoins to protect the house's corners and dressed stone was also set at intervals in broad expanses of masonry to increase its stability (fig 4).

Pebbles *(galets)* gathered from river beds and set into mortar were used for walling in areas where stone was scarce. The availability of lime mortar greatly increased this practice. Sometimes a decorative fern pattern was used with bands of flat bricks interposed to give the walls additional strength. Combining different materials, composite walling, also included the use of chalk and flint or brick (fig 5) often attractively patterned, while brick on its own was laid in rows according to an established 'bond' (fig 6). But brick was rare in farmhouses before 1850 because of the expense of burning it.

2. In some houses transversely-laid stones protrude beyond the walls.

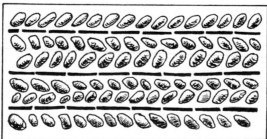

3. The outer face of many older walls leans slightly inwards.

4. Dressed stone was used for quoins and to strengthen walls.

5. Composite walling made of mixed materials.

6. Top: brick bonds using old brick: running, Flemish and a variation of English bond.

43

WOOD AND EARTHEN WALLS

Pan de bois, literally 'piece of wood', refers mainly to constructions in which a jointed timber frame forms the skeleton of a building (fig 1). In mountainous regions, where wood was fairly abundant, a cladding of planks was sometimes nailed to the inner and outer faces of the timber frame (fig 2). Tobacco barns are another example of this technique, using weatherboarding. But the method that has become synonymous with *pan de bois* – and produced its most aesthetic

2. *Some timber frames were clad with planks.*

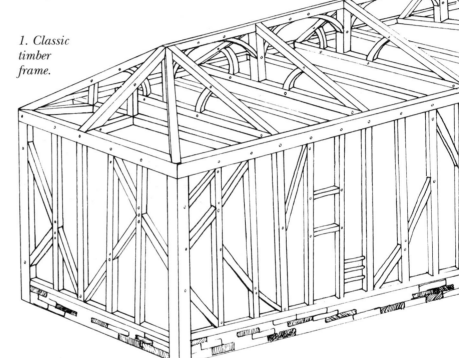

1. *Classic timber frame.*

3. *Mortice and tenon joints.*

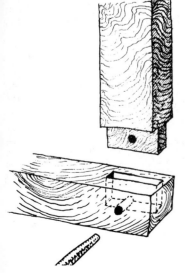

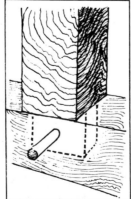

Simple joint

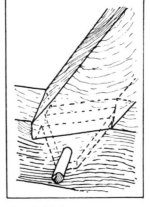

Angled joint

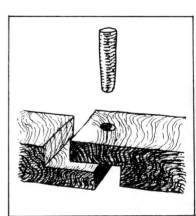

'Mi-bois' joint

expression – is half timbering or *colombage,* where the timber frame is infilled with wattle and daub or bricks. Normandy, Alsace, Bresse, Champagne and the Landes all contain fine examples.

Surprisingly, timber frames can sometimes be found in the fabric of older stone houses and this may show a lack of confidence in changing to stone from the familiar medium of wattle and daub. But building a roof supported by a timber frame also meant that mud-mortared walls were shielded from wet weather during construction.

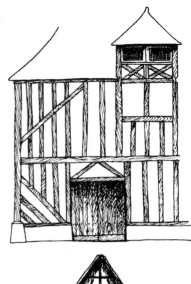

TIMBER FRAMES were joined by mortice and tenon joints (fig 3), an interlocking system in which a wooden peg *(cheville)* penetrates a socket joint and pins two pieces of wood together.

Timber frame walls comprise an upper and lower beam attached to a corner post, as shown in fig 1. The lower beam rests on a masonry foundation, but it is the corner posts, not the foundations, that carry the weight.

In *colombage,* a row of thinner posts *(potelets)* was placed between the horizontal beams, their spacing and arrangement dependent on local tradition (fig 4). Some were set vertically, others obliquely or in an X called a St André's cross. But all increased support, while at the same time acting as anchors for infill.

Where there was a second storey, an additional horizontal beam was placed at ceiling level.

Framing timbers were usually numbered in Roman numerals and a trial assembly was not uncommon, especially if timbers had to be carried to the building site. The timbers were assembled on the ground one side at a time, then the sides were raised and, eventually, joined together.

4. Arrangement of timber posts is key to local style.

5. Torchis *applied to sticks embedded in upright timbers.*

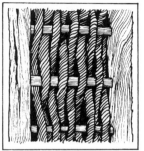

6. *Straw rope woven over trellis is typical of the Landes.*

7. *Brick infill was an alternative to wattle and daub.*

INFILL *Torchis* was applied to a 'trellis' erected between the secondary posts *(potelets)* (fig 5). Short sticks were embedded in grooves or holes on the inner sides of the posts. Sometimes lath was used and sometimes hazel branches or mud-soaked ropes of straw were woven over the 'trellis' (fig. 6), then the *torchis* mixture was trowelled or hand-pressed on to both sides to the width of the supporting posts, or very nearly.

When dry, the wall was plastered inside and out with mud or lime plaster *(enduit* or *crépi)*, and might be whitewashed afterwards.

Colombage required considerable skill and it has been estimated that a house with a thatched roof required some 15 tonnes of clay soil and about 1000 litres of water; it would take six men working ten hours a day a month to construct.

Brick was used as infill instead of *torchis* mainly in the late 19th century. It was laid in attractive obliquely set patterns (fig 7) or, occasionally, plastered over.

BANCHAGE This ancient form of rammed earth construction using *pisé* originated in the Middle East and, like so much else, is thought to have been introduced into France during the Roman occupation.

Pisé (the material used in *banchage)* is strong and it does not absorb humidity or salts. But like all clay mixtures, *pisé* is vulnerable to water – also to rodents. For this reason walls were erected, as for *torchis,* on a low masonry foundation. But unlike *torchis, pisé* is freestanding.

The mixture, generally containing gravel, was loaded between two oiled wood shutters held together by crosspieces and cotter pins (fig 8), then tamped down with a wooden pestle, and by feet. Usually two men worked inside the mould and two outside. By filling it only a few inches at a time and compacting the *pisé* to about half its size before adding more, an even compression was achieved.

When the mould was full of pounded earth, the shutters were removed and re-erected to form the adjacent block. The cross pieces were either left to rot or hacked back and the holes then filled with plaster.

By slightly overlapping previous blocks, the shutters enabled a firm bond to be made, the *pisé* usually doubling as a mortar. In the Auvergne and Lyonnais however lime mortar was used and the blocks often had angled joins (see photo on page 28).

When one course was laid, it was possible to go straight to the next, but an overall drying period of two or three months was necessary before walls could be roofed.

Window and door openings were made during construction by erecting temporary framing timbers to the required dimensions.

The finished walls were normally rendered and/or limewashed.

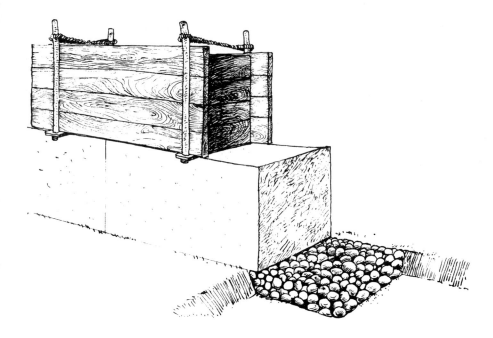

8. In banchage *huge 'bricks' are moulded in situ using a stiff clay mixture,* pisé. *(The word* pisé *comes from Latin* pinsare *'to beat'.)*

A reasonably unskilled technique, *banchage* could be undertaken by local peasants with little or no supervision. Two men are said to have been able to build about one cubic yard of rammed earth walls per day. The technique was much used in the Garonne valley, western Dauphiné and parts of Lyonnais and the Auvergne.

ADOBE, described under Materials, was laid like bricks and bound by mortar of the same stuff it was made of. Adobe also formed part of composite walls and, being light, was sometimes used on the upper level of stonebuilt houses and barns in for example the southwest. Adobe brick walls were normally rendered.

BAUGE differs from *torchi*s and *pisé* in that the clay consisted of lumps or large balls often loaded on to walls with a pitchfork and hand-packed in rows. When a layer was completed it was smoothed down with a knife and the top covered with straw. A week later, when the clay had dried, the next layer was added, often on top of the straw.

INTERIOR WALLS

Supporting walls (*murs de refend*) were built of the same material as exterior walls, and finished like them. Partition walls (*cloisons*) on the other hand were often very thin, constructed of wood panelling or a narrow row of bricks.

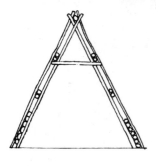

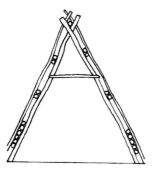

1. Early crucks were both wall timbers and roof.

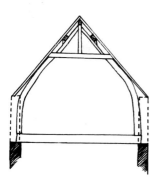

2. In raised cruck construction the cruck was mounted on a wall, making a spacious loft.

ROOFS AND ROOFING

Roof style represents the strongest architectural divide in France. The south is roofed almost exclusively in rounded canal tiles set on broad, low-pitched roofs to keep them from slipping off. This ancient Mediterranean practice is in sharp contrast with the steeply sloping roofs of the north that, covered with slates and flat tiles, were originally designed for thatch. The border between the two main types roughly approximates a line drawn between St Malo and Geneva, and reflects the old medieval boundaries of *langue d'oc* and *langue d'oïl*, each with a flourishing language and culture. But as the map shows, both blocks have pockets of the other's roofs: canal tiles are found in Lorraine, while flat tiles crop up near the Pyrénées in Beárn and in Périgord-Quercy. The reason for these discrepancies is unknown. Roman routes have been suggested for Lorraine; also migrations of peoples and, in particular, of craftsmen. Probably the answer is all three.

CONSTRUCTION The central challenge of roofing is to build a cover with maximum free space underneath. In France two principal methods developed early on; the first and more primitive was the cruck.

Crucks. In cruck roofs (fig 1) the rafters spring as it were from the ground, making an arch overhead. The technique probably derived from bending pairs of saplings and tying them together as a frame for brush or bracken covering. Crucks can span wide areas but the naturally curved timbers best-suited to make an arch were also needed by shipbuilders, who had priority. Crucks also require very long timbers, another rarity; and not surprisingly the style began to die out in the Middle Ages.

But the raised cruck (fig 2), a variation, continued to thrive. In this form the arched timbers were erected on a low wall. Raised crucks were popular throughout the north and west of France and they continued to be built in the poorer areas of Limousin and Brittany into the 19th century. The technique could be used for buildings of up to one and a half storeys, creating lofts unimpeded by posts or struts, and so ideal for storage; but the method was useless in two-storeyed construction. Besides, crucks' chief advantage had been their ability to take the roof load straight to the ground. As walls improved and were able to do this, crucks – even raised crucks – became redundant, the latter blurring into a system better-suited for roofing loadbearing walls: the truss.

Aisled halls. The antecedents of trusses are found in 'aisled halls' (fig 3) where roof timbers rest on one or two rows of freestanding posts, creating aisles between. Seen in barns, churches and above all market halls,

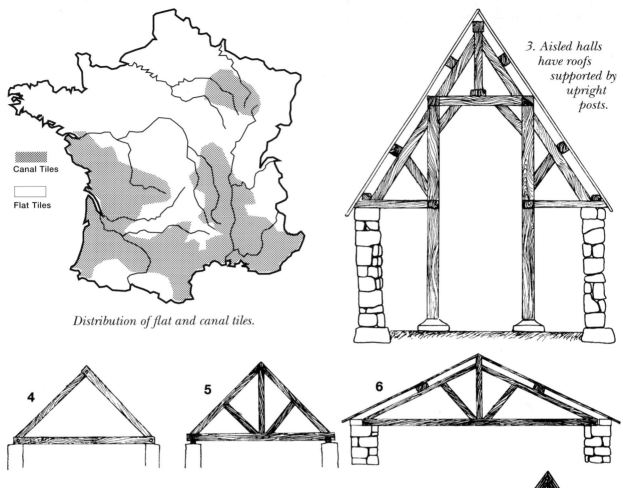

Distribution of flat and canal tiles.

3. Aisled halls
have roofs
supported by
upright
posts.

Canal Tiles

Flat Tiles

4

5

6

7

farmhouses constructed in this manner exist in Champagne, Burgundy, Lorraine and parts of southwest France; also in Alpine regions.

But posts restricted free circulation and it was but one step to remove them to the perimeters of a building, leaving the floor space free. This was made possible by trusses.

Trussed roofs. Roof trusses *(fermes)* are triangles made of two 'blades' joined at the bottom by a tie beam (fig 4). Theoretically indeformable, they guaranteed the support of considerable weight. The tie beam helped to counter outward pressure on walls and could double as a joist to support the ceiling. But heavy timbers were needed and, with heavy roofing materials, underpinning – which took up space. Various underpinning methods were used.

Kingposts (poinçons), were the most usual mode, often reinforced with struts, (fig 5). Popular from the 13th century, kingpost and upper kingpost roofs (see below) are typical of old houses in the north and west. A squat version (fig 6), ubiquitous in the south, supports the low, tiled roofs which, like the kingpost, were a Roman legacy.

Collar ties (entraits retroussés) are a variation in which the tie beam is raised to create more room (fig 7). And some French roofs have both (fig

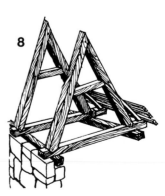

8

4 - 8. Trussed roofs
with their various
supports.

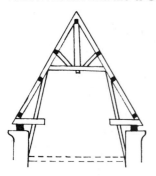

9. Trussed roofs with side struts are common in steeply-sloped roofs of the north.

8). Collar ties can also be strengthened by kingposts and/or reinforced from the sides by struts called *jambes de force* and *blochets* (fig 9). The latter created considerable overhead space and numerous examples can be seen, especially in steeply-pitched roofs of the north.

Purlins (pannes). A fourth type of trussed roof is the purlin roof, in which longitudinal timbers, the purlins, are laid from gable to gable on top of trusses (fig 10a). (Occasionally the trusses were omitted and the purlins supported by the gables). Developed in the 13th century, purlin roofs came into general use about 200 years later. To prevent bending, purlins need to be placed within two metres of one another, but by adding a collar tie to the truss this distance could be doubled. Purlins were not necessarily single timbers: many were spliced together at the trusses.

Double rafter roofs (fermes à pannes). From the Middle Ages, the biggest challenge facing carpenters was working with smaller and smaller bits of wood and, in the 18th century, an important innovation appeared, greatly reducing the need for heavy timbers. The double rafter roof had rafters on top of the purlins (fig 10b). Sometimes a ridgepole was added but more often pairs of rafters were pegged together at the apex.

10a. Purlin roof timbers are laid across trusses.

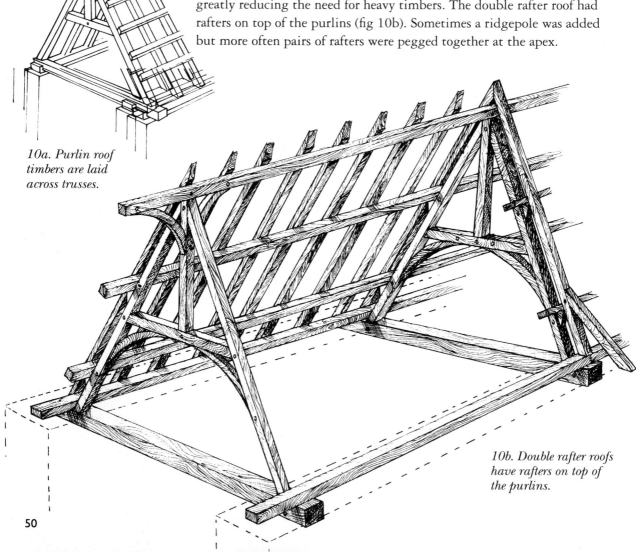

10b. Double rafter roofs have rafters on top of the purlins.

ROOF STYLES Farmhouse roofs were either two-sloped with gable ends (*pignons*) or were hipped (*croupe*) – the latter being of greater antiquity.

Constructed by splaying the end truss (fig 11a), hipped roofs are found all over France. They lend themselves to coverings of thatch and tiles, while gable roofs, the result of improved walling methods in the Middle Ages, can also accommodate stone and slate. It is not unusual for some buildings to have a hip at one end and a gable at the other.

Demi-croupes or *croupettes* are another combination of hip and gable: the snub-nosed hip perching on half a gable (fig 11b). Found in many regions, they are very often seen on barns. *Demi-croupes* are constructed like hipped roofs, but on a smaller scale.

In the 17th century an elegant variation of hipped roofs, the mansard, was designed in France (fig 12). Each side has two slopes, the lower one being taller and steeper. Chiefly seen in towns, mansards found their way into the countryside in the 18th century, their vast attics making them desirable for storage.

The pavilion roof is a steep, hipped roof in which all four slopes are the same dimensions (fig 13). The style is often seen on dovecotes.

Incurving is a feature of many older roofs and does not indicate sagging. Its purpose is to increase watertightness, the curve causing tiles to lie more securely against the ones beneath (fig 14). Incurving also helps to throw water away from the walls.

Alterations Many old roofs were adapted in the 19th century to suit new covering and, where slates replaced thatch, it was not unusual to reduce the angle of slope by raising the walls a metre or so.

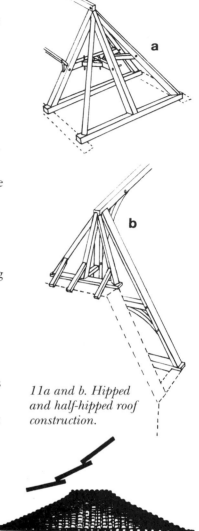

11a and b. Hipped and half-hipped roof construction.

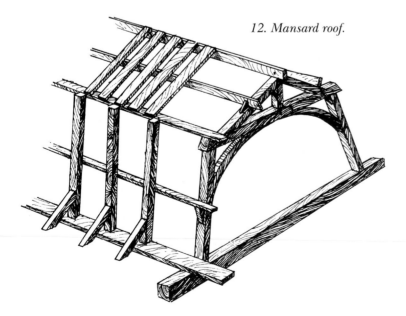

12. Mansard roof.

14. Incurving improves watertightness.

13. Pavilion roof.

CORNICES Gutters were rarely used on farmhouses and the water streamed down on all sides, increasing the problems posed by rising damp. Not surprisingly, present-day owners tend to counter this by adding a gutter system, even if it means obscuring a cornice designed (if less effectively) to cast water off and keep the walls dry.

The oldest method of keeping water away from walls was an overhanging roof, made by extending the roof rafters (fig 15). The effect is like the brim of a hat and examples exist all over France. Cornices served the same purpose. They were made by thickening the upper wall (fig 16) or, more usually, adding a decorative ledge (fig 17). Wood, masonry, tiles and, in parts of Provence, plaster of Paris, were all employed; the style being dictated by local tradition.

Génoises are a type of cornice peculiar to the south. They comprise one to three rows of canal tiles embedded in the walls, often with a band of

15. Overhanging eaves are the oldest means of keeping water off walls.

16-17. Cornices were made by thickening upper walls or adding a decorative ledge.

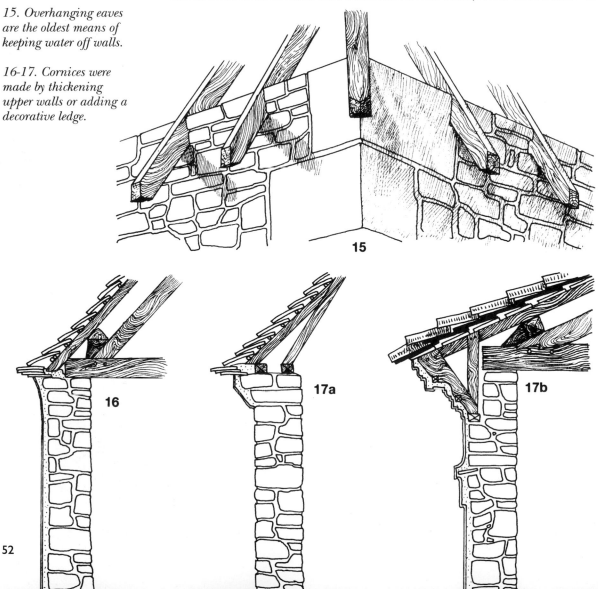

15

16

17a

17b

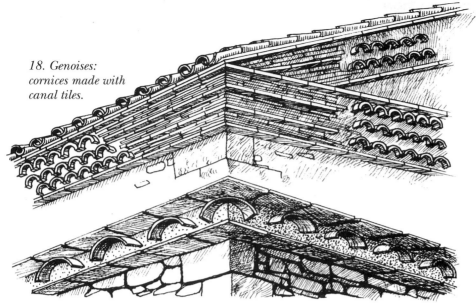

18. Genoises: cornices made with canal tiles.

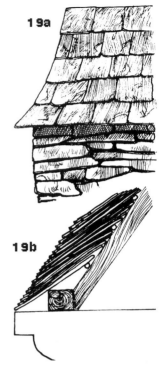

19a

19b

19c

19. Often adopted during conversion from thatch, coyaux jettisoned water by means of a steep curve.

flat tiles in between (fig 18). The effect is a sort of 'dogteeth' and the number of rows reflected a building's importance. Corner treatment varied, some *génoises* stopping short of the corner (Guyenne), and others rounding it (Provence).

Coyaux are yet another means of jettisoning water, mainly from flat tiles or slates. The roof pitch, descending in a straight line suddenly curves outward at the bottom (fig 19a). This curve is the *coyau* and it works something like a children's slide. It has been suggested the *coyaux* developed when thatched roofs (fig 19b) were abandoned for slates and tiles, as a means of making up the difference between a thinner roofing material and the thick walls (fig 19c).

EPIS It was the custom in some regions to ornament roof ridges with a variety of upright motifs. *Epis* were moulded in terracotta, iron or lead, or carved in stone; they are one of the few examples in peasant houses of decoration often for its own sake (though many *épis* cover the joins on roofs). Motifs vary from small repeat designs along the roof ridge to figures like giant chessmen standing sentinel on the gable ends (fig 20).

20. Epis covered joins and at the same time decorated rooftops.

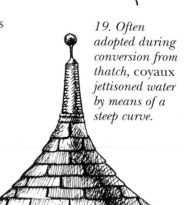

ROOFING Thatch, slates, tiles and stone slabs were the traditional materials for roofing. Geology, the roof slope and local custom dictated which was used. The covering material was attached to battens or planks on the roof timbers (fig 1). This undercover or *volige* helped to steady the trusses and distribute the roof load evenly for, compared with modern materials, traditional covering was heavy: up to 45kg per m2 for hand-split slates and 100kg per m2 for stone slabs.

　　Thatch *(chaume)*, comparatively rare today, was in the 18th century the traditional roofing for over half the country. Readily available, it only needed to be thickly applied to keep out rain, and its isometric qualities were excellent. The drawbacks were rot – steep roof pitches were needed so that water could run off quickly – and fire. The latter caused its demise. This happened early in towns, where numerous edicts were issued against thatching, but in the country its popularity continued into the 19th century, when slates and tiles became economically competitive as replacements.

1. Roof covering was attached to either battens or planks.

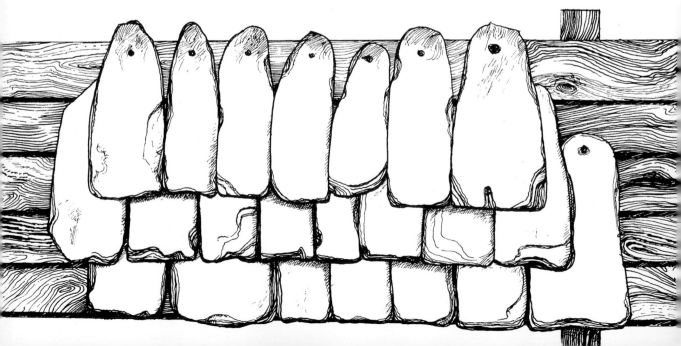

2. Some thatch was tied directly to purlins and held down on top by poles.

3. Thatch was also tied to poles, themselves tied to the purlins.

Straw, normally rye, was cut in August. During the winter the sheaves were beaten and the straw gathered into bundles about a metre thick. Modes of attaching varied: in the Dauphiné the bundles were tied directly to the purlins (fig 2). In Brittany the bundles were tied to poles which were themselves tied to the purlins (fig 3), and in the Auvergne thatch was stitched. Methods of securing edges differed too: earth or lime mortar was applied in Normandy and Brittany, where it is customary to seed a row of irises *en épi* along the mortared ridge. In the Auvergne and Dauphiné the straw poked up in a bushy crest along the ridge line.

Water reed *(roseau),* popular along the coastal marshlands, was cut in September and October, when rain made the stems more pliable. The bundles, laid on poplar battens and tied with osier branches, were arranged so that only the butt ends of stalks were exposed (fig 4). The water was shed from tip to tip. An average cottage roof required some 2500 bundles of reed and five kilometres of hemp to join them.

Thatching never disappeared in remoter areas like the Grand Brière (Brittany), and in Normandy it is enjoying a comeback: many old cottages, called *chaumières* because of once-thatched roofs, have been lovingly restored as second homes, and have had their thatch put back.

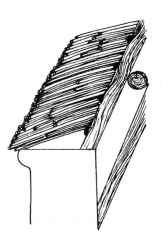

4. Water reed roofing has stalk ends exposed.

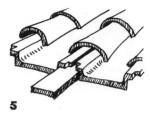

5

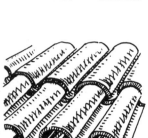

6

Canal tiles *(tuiles canal).* These unglazed half-cylinders are often known misleadingly as Roman tiles. But Roman tiling had a flat lower tile with a lip (fig 5): only the top tiles were curved and it is this tile that seems to have survived, fulfilling the functions of both. A few Roman-style tiled roofs can still be found in the Massif Central (Puy-de-Dôme), Champagne, Lorraine and the southwest. But in most places the style died out in the Middle Ages.

A canal-tiled roof is in effect a system of vertical gutters. And as terracotta does not absorb heat, the roof also repulses the sun. The tiles,

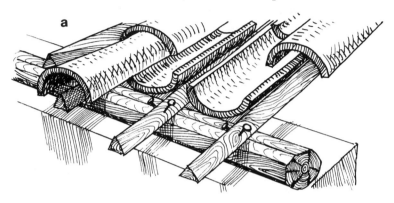

5. Top: Roman-tiled roofs have flat lower tiles.

6. Above: half-cylinder canal tiles typical of the south have one end larger than the other.

7. Canal tiles were laid on vertical battens (a) or horizontal planks (b).

8. The bottom row of tiles often formed gutter spouts.

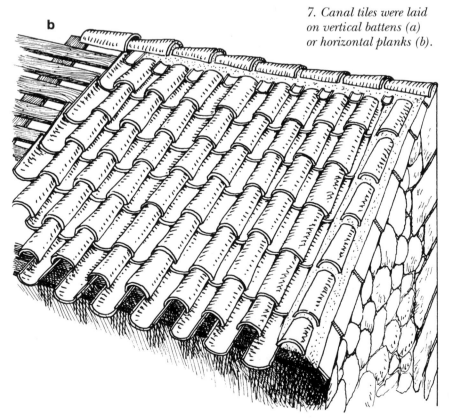

larger at one end than the other (fig 6) to prevent slipping, vary somewhat in size in different regions: the smallest are found in Lorraine and the largest in Provence and Languedoc.

Canal tiles were made on convex wooden moulds and were usually laid on roofs either on top of planks or on triangular wood battens attached vertically to the purlins (fig 7). The roof edges were sealed with mortar. (An exception was at Baugé, see Loire.) In the southwest, a bottom row of tiles often projected beyond the roof in a series of tiny spouts, a charming and probably very ancient custom (fig 8).

Many canal-tiled roofs are hipped and, when the end slopes are fairly steep, flat tiles are used to cover them (fig 9).

9. Many canal-tiled roofs have flat-tiled hips or croupes.

Stone slabs *(lauzes)*. This old and very beautiful mode of roofing goes by several names: for example, *laves* in Burgundy and *platins* in the west. Suggestive of heavy, armour-plated fossils, many are over 200 years old and still in pristine condition.

Limestone and schist were the main types of stone used for roofing and strong timbers were needed to support them. Schist, a layered rock, splits easily, and much of the work was accomplished by simply leaving the stone to weather during the winter. The action of frost along the cleaving lines split the rock naturally and finishing could then be done by hand.

Slabs were usually pierced and attached to roofing planks with hardwood pegs, the largest stones placed along the lower edge. In windy regions like the Cotentin (Normandy), however, plaques were sealed with mortar, while Burgundian *laves* had pebbles wedged underneath the slabs to keep them in place (fig 10).

Stone slab roofs remain a distinctive feature of the Auvergne, Alps, Manche, Burgundy and Anjou.

10. Pebbles wedged between stone slabs kept them in place; alternatively slabs were pegged or sealed with mortar.

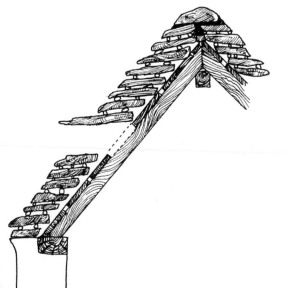

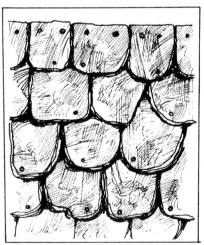

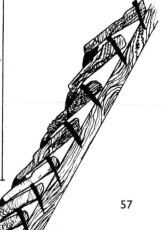

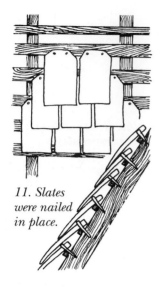

11. Slates were nailed in place.

12. Fishtail slates.

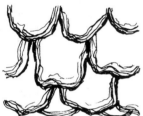

13. Mode of sealing slate ridgeline.

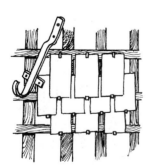

14. Modern slates are attached by metal hook.

Slates (*ardoises*) are a thinner, more tailored form of stone slabs. Made from schist, slates were split into layers of uniform thickness using a hammer and chisel. A thickness of one centimetre was average but this varied and it is the stubby irregularity of old slate roofs that gives them much of their charm.

Slate roofs first appeared in the Middle Ages but they did not arrive in the countryside till much later, and then only in areas like Anjou, where supplies were plentiful. Improved transport in the 19th century however made slate an answer to volatile thatch. The slates were delivered in bulk and the biggest pulled out first for use lower down on the roof. Nailed to roofing planks (fig 11), some slates had rounded bottom edges like fish scales (fig 12) and, glistening in the sun after a rainstorm, the effect is remarkably convincing.

It was customary to seal slate ridgelines with a row of canal tiles or, in many older houses, by interlocking slates *en lignolet* (fig 13).

Modern slates, split by machine, are thinner and rather monotonous, covering old roofs in what is generally too smooth a skin. The slates are attached to roof battens by a metal hook, the tip of which remains visible (fig 14). In Caux, for example, where large square slates are hooked on the roof at an angle, the diamond pattern produced goes a long way to relieve the monotony.

Slate was quarried in a number of regions: the Loire, Anjou, Brittany, Cotentin and Caux, and in parts of the Alps, the Ardennes and Bigorre. It is also found in Cantal and the Auvergne, where graded slates can still be seen on many older houses.

Shingles (*bardeaux*) were once in common usage throughout Europe. In France oak, beech and chestnut were preferred and, in mountainous regions, larch and fir. In many cases, the heartwood of a tree could be used for framing timber and the outer sapwood split to make the shingles. Sizes

15. Alpine plank roofing.

varied from 30cm to over a metre in length. In parts of the Alps, for example, pine planks *(ancelles)* some 80cm long were used (fig 15). At higher altitudes, where roofs were often steeper, shorter *tavaillons* about 50cm were nailed on the roof battens or on the wind-exposed side of houses. The difficulty of repairing them however widened the use of *ancelles*.

Sometimes shingles were given rounded ends or laid in decorative patterns.

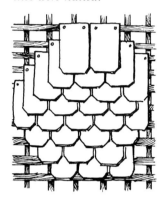

16b. Round-ended flat tiles were nailed.

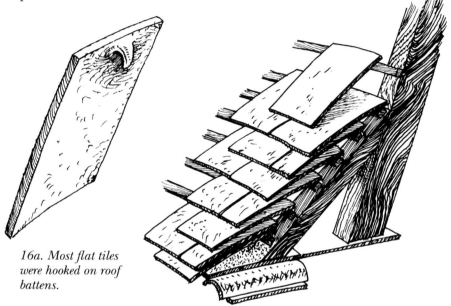

16a. Most flat tiles were hooked on roof battens.

17. A row of canal tiles capped flat-tiled ridges.

Flat tiles *(tuiles plates)* are thought to have originated in the Orient. They first appeared in France, probably from Flanders, in the 12th or 13th century as fireproof substitutes for thatch and shingles. Two types were dominant: the squared edge had a spur which was hooked on to the roof battens (fig 16a). The curved edge was nailed (fig 16b). It was customary to overlap tiles by 2/3, creating a triple thickness.

Gable ends were sealed with lime mortar and the roof ridge capped by a row of mortared canal tiles (fig 17).

Flat tiles are found in Ile de France and Normandy, Burgundy, Champagne, Berry, the Dordogne and in Beárn on roofs with slopes of between 40-55 degrees.

Pantiles *(pannes à flamande)* are peculiar to Flanders and Picardy, though outside France their use extends along the North Sea coast as far as Scandinavia. S-shaped, pantiles overlap laterally (fig 18) and were attached by hooks to the roof battens. (Modern mechanical tiles are similar but very thick and of a raw colour.)

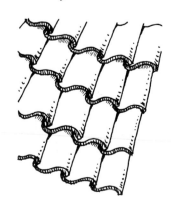

18. Pantiles overlap laterally as well as vertically.

1. *The three categories of window;* fenêtre, lucarne, jour.

WINDOWS & DOORS

Windows and doors are, next to shape, easily the most important feature in a building's appearance. They create focus and rhythm and their treatment, especially in simpler houses, often gives a dwelling its main character. Window groupment and size, and the type or style of surround, are important considerations – as of course are light and ventilation.

In very old houses there may be only one window or, as in Normandy, an outside door for every room; yet the spatial relationship is always pleasing. It has been suggested that classical values are responsible – and they may play a part – but a similar harmony is found in vernacular buildings throughout the world. Peasant dress showed a similar awareness.

WINDOWS in France fall into three main categories: ordinary windows (*fenêtres*), dormers (*lucarnes*) and small 'spotlight' windows or oculi known as *jours*, used for lighting areas like stairs and outbuildings (fig 1).

Windows are one of the few instances where significant technical improvements occurred after the Middle Ages. As a result, few older houses have their original windows. A growing awareness of hygiene (activated by a flood of pamphlets), the desire for more light and less draught, and improved agricultural prosperity, contributed to a large-scale modernisation of windows in the 18th and 19th centuries. But older windows still exist, a rewarding vision to the sharpened eye.

Medieval windows were normally square or horizontal (fig 2), the opening divided into panels by stone or wooden mullions. Heavily oiled paper or cloth was stretched across the window to make a protective and translucent membrane. Some houses had one or two slit windows (fig 3), a

Right: Normandy window's vertical wooden bar suggests earlier medieval styles.

2

3

2-5 Early window styles: lead panes, slit, wood bars, metal grills.

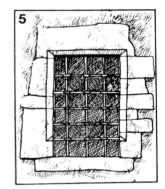

5

reminder of the continual warfare waged in France before the 17th century.

Much more common however were windows with vertical wooden bars (fig 4) or, in wealthier houses, iron grills (fig 5). The former continued in use well into the 19th century, while basket grills can still be seen in a number of larger Breton farmhouses.

Glass panes first appeared in houses 300 years ago. Small, fragile and extremely thin, panes were joined by leading, like stained glass, to form a panel (see fig 2). But by the end of the 18th century, glass makers were producing panes large enough to span a whole panel. This advance paralleled a change from horizontal to a vertical window shape, that allowed more light to enter a room. The classic French window (fig 6) had arrived: two-panelled, six or eight panes (occasionally more) per window, and opening inwards. (Foreigners' idea of French windows, i.e. glass *doors,*

6. Classic French farmhouse window outside and in.

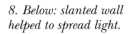

7. Openings were reinforced by lintels and arches, and given stone, brick or wood surrounds.

a   b

were never used in farmhouses for the simple reason that there were too many animals about.)

Window openings. Making a hole in masonry weakens the wall; therefore the area above the hole must be supported. Generally, a stone and/or oak lintel (fig 7a) was employed, or a peaked masonry arch (fig 7b) built above the lintel. In wealthier medieval establishments the area below the window was used to make a window seat – and make the window itself easier to get at (see fig 2). Eventually the practice arose of keeping the area under the window flush (fig 8) and slanting the surrounding edges to help spread the light. This is the treatment most often seen today.

It was easier to make openings in half-timbered houses since the 'surrounds' could be fitted into the overall frame of the building (fig 9)

Windows had no ledges but sills sloped slightly downwards to dispel the rain.

8. Below: slanted wall helped to spread light.

9. Wooden window surrounds were part of timber frame.

Dormers *(lucarnes)* were designed to give access and/or ventilation to lofts. Approached by a ladder from outside, they usually had a wooden door. (Interior stairs evolved for added convenience, especially where the loft, or part of it, was used for sleeping.)

Dormers are of two types, depending on whether they are set entirely or only partly in the roof: respectively *lucarnes fenêtres* and *lucarnes portes* (fig 10). Dormers have had a significant role in vernacular style, their decorative aspects having been inspired by the stylistic importance given them in Renaissance chateaux.

10. Dormers could either be set in the roof or partly so.

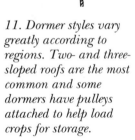

11. Dormer styles vary greatly according to regions. Two- and three-sloped roofs are the most common and some dormers have pulleys attached to help load crops for storage.

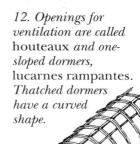

12. Openings for ventilation are called houteaux *and one-sloped dormers,* lucarnes rampantes. *Thatched dormers have a curved shape.*

Usually dormer roofs have either two or three slopes, the pitch being that of the main roof. Many two-sloped dormers have imposing surrounds or *frontons* of dressed stone, while those with three-slopes *(lucarnes à capucine),* popular in Normandy and Ile de France, sometimes have a projected awning with a pulley to lift up crops.

One-sloped dormers do exist; also small openings known as *houteaux,* (fig 12) that give air but not accessibility. Thatched dormers could also be called 'one-sloped' since the square windows are framed by an arch of thatch.

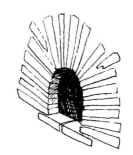

Jours. These often tiny openings (fig 13) bring light and ventilation to cellars, stairs, lofts, kitchen sinks and the upper levels of one-and-a-half storey houses. When combined with ordinary windows, they create a gracefully graduated symmetrical facade (fig 14). *Jours* have a variety of shapes: bulls-eyes, lozenges, rectangles and semi-circles; some have panes and some do not.

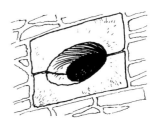

14. *Jours greatly enhanced symmetrical facades.*

13. *Above: types of* jours *set into walls for light or ventilation.*

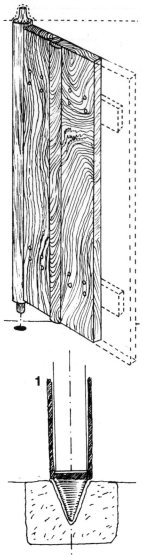

1. Left: pivoting door sockets are seen in barns today.

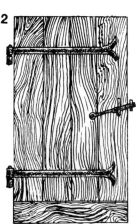

2. Strap-hinged door.

DOORS *(portes)* were the main source of light and air, and many were kept open all day. Indeed a closed door in the daytime usually signified suspect goings on inside.

But in earlier, more turbulent times doors had to resist battering. Two nail-studded layers of planks, one horizontal and one vertical; or a single layer nailed on battens, was everywhere the style. A plank across the bottom of the door, as shown above, helped protect the main panel from wear and this 'kickboard' remained typical of country doors into the present century.

Many early doors turned on sockets of stone or wood (fig 1), a practice still used for some barn doors. Long strap hinges (fig 2) were the alternative.

Some doors divided transversely, like stable doors, so that the top could be left opened and farmyard animals kept out.

In the 19th century doors became taller and, in order to light the newly introduced passage or vestibule, doorways were surmounted by a three-light transom *(imposte)*. Later on, glass panes were inserted in the door itself, a practice that filtered out from towns, where security was less a problem than in more isolated spots. Doors of two leaves were also popular and some doors had a small hinged panel for peering through.

Doorways were usually square-headed under a lintel of wood or stone; but arches, a Renaissance feature, offered a graceful alternative.

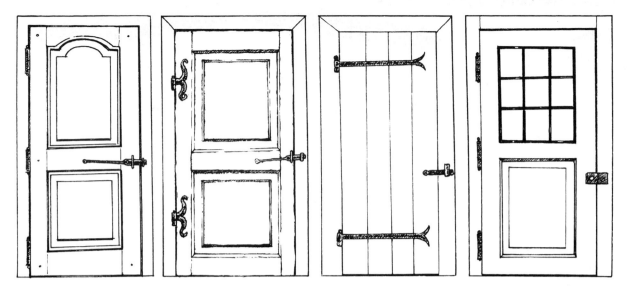

Interior doors were simple panels to begin with, but the development of framed panelling in the 16th century sparked a change that eventually found its way into the humblest cottage. But whatever the arrangement of panels, and whether or not they were chamfered, one panel was nearly always square.

Doors were constructed of either planks or panelling. Glass-paned exterior doors became popular because they let in light when closed.

SHUTTERS (*volets*) Early shutters opened inwards or were removable, but panelled frames made it possible to hinge two or three together so that they folded neatly back against the wall. In modest houses however shutters began to be put outside, a move made possible by improved mortars that made it easier to embed hinges; also by the development of sturdier paints.

Exterior shutters were constructed, like early front doors, of planks nailed on battens (fig 1a). Oblique supports (where used) helped to shift weight towards the hinges (fig 1b). In Provence two layers of planks were

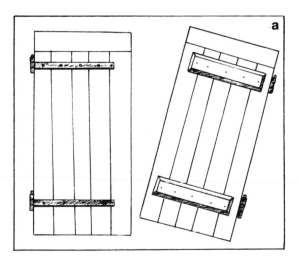
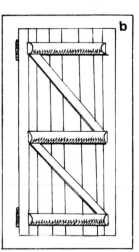

1a and b. Shutters, like early doors, were planks nailed on battens.

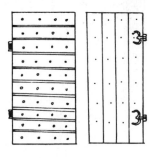

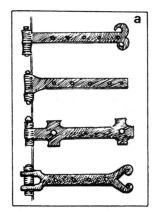

Provençal shutters made of two layers of planks. In other regions a cut-out or peephole in the shutters might let in a patch of light.

1. Strap hinges (a, b), split hinge (c) and jointed hinge (d).

sometimes used, or the planks were nailed on a wooden frame. Some shutters had a *portisol,* an Italian idea that let in a patch of light when the shutters were closed. In other places – Alsace for instance – this was done by cutting out a motif.

Louvred shutters *(persiennes),* to many minds synonymous with French houses, were rarely used in the countryside, becoming popular in towns in the 18th century.

HARDWARE *(ferrage)* Strap hinges *(pentures à gonds)* for windows and doors (fig 1a, b) were nailed and their supports embedded in the masonry; but the development of wooden surrounds for doors and windows called for smaller hinges – made possible by the 19th century proliferation of metal screws. At about the same time, a decorative split hinge or piano hinge *(paumelle)* appeared (fig 1c). It was used extensively on furniture as well as windows and doors. The jointed hinge *(fiche)* (fig 1d) also came into use in the 19th century, allowing shutters and doors to be removed at will.

Locking and closing were accomplished in simpler houses by a wooden bar *(fléau).* Attached to the window (fig 2), it could be easily pivoted into place. A similar version was used for shutters and, of course, on doors.

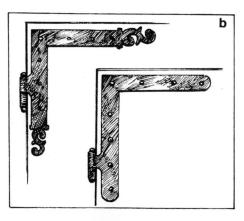

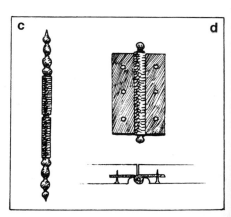

Sliding bolts (fig 3a) and metal pivots operated by a half turn were also popular; but it was the *espagnolette* (fig 3b) that revolutionized window treatment, enabling windows to be opened and closed in one easy motion. An improved version, the *crémone* (fig 3c) appeared at the beginning of this century, but *espagnolettes* remained in use for shutters. Small, often S-shaped metal pieces called *tourillons* held the open shutters against the outside wall (fig 4).

In poorer houses latches continued to be made of wood, but delicately wrought metal versions (fig 5) enjoyed a wide early 20th century popularity. They can sometimes be bought today in antique shops.

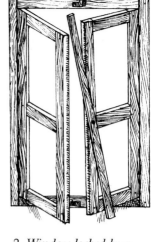

2. *Window locked by a pivoting bar.*

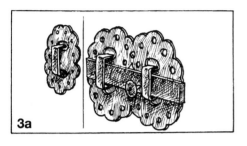

4. *Left: S-shaped* tourillons *secured open shutters.*

5. *Below: typical French latches.*

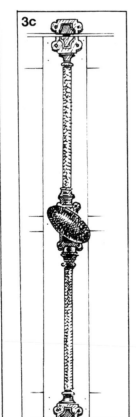

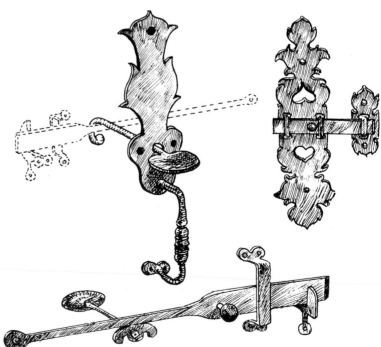

3. *Bolts for door (a), shutters (b), windows (c).*

FLOORS

Farmhouse floors used to be beaten earth *(terre battue)*. In a few better-off houses, however, stone flags *(dalles)* were put down, with impressive effect; and in the north, especially in Normandy, brick was sometimes used, laid in pleasing herringbone patterns. Wood floors *(parquet)*, though occasionally installed downstairs, were normally found in the loft.

In the late 19th century, the spread of *tuileries* enabled clay tiles to be 'mass-produced' and flat, unglazed tiles began to be laid in bedrooms and parlours (where they existed) – though many kitchens or *salles* retained their traditional beaten earth.

Beaten earth produces a hard, burnished surface; but enough water coming in under doors, or by tracking feet (chickens and pigs came in as well as people), turned the floor into a mudbath. Moreover, beaten earth pockmarks easily and furniture often needed a wedge to keep it steady. (The disfigured feet on many rustic antiques are due to the humidity of earthen floors.)

'Beating' was not especially onerous, involving as it did mixing a little lime or straw into the moistened soil, uncorking the cider jug and throwing a dancing party – the livelier the better. And every few years, *grace à Dieu,* the floor needed a retread. Earthen floors are not entirely things of the past: they can still be found in Brittany (though most have been replaced by poured concrete).

Terracotta tiles *(terre cuite)* or quarry tiles are unglazed tiles made of clay and a little lime, and cooked at a low temperature (900c). Moulded in rectangles, squares and hexagons, they vary in size from 32cm square in the Garonne valley to the tiny Provençal hexagons known as *malons* or *tomettes.* Their colours – ochre, red and a warm leathery brown – depended on the soil. (These tiles should not be confused with glazed tiles which were never used for flooring.)

Tiles were laid close together on a bed of earth, sand or lime mortar; but normally the joints were left dry, the under-edges having been carefully bevelled to assure a close fit.

Tile flooring is known collectively as *carrelage.* (For information on laying and caring for tiles, see the Appendix).

CEILINGS

In builders' parlance, *plancher* refers to the carrying members of a ceiling (or floor); the flooring itself is the *sol.* In many older houses, tie beams (part of the roof trusses) performed the role of *plancher.* If a room did not exceed four metres, the alternative was to lay a row of joists *(solives)* from

1. Beams laid across walls supported loft floor and were left exposed underneath.

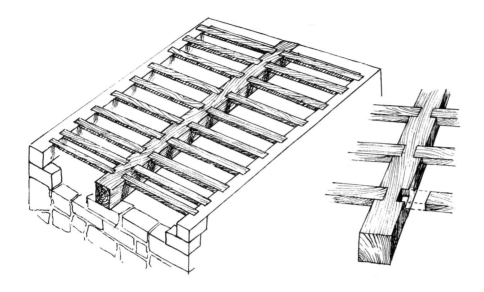

2. A central beam was needed to support ceiling timbers in large rooms.

wall to wall (fig 1). In larger rooms joists were further supported by one or two beams *(poutres),* and sometimes embedded in the top of them (fig 2). This method is called *'à la francaise'.*

Entire trees were at one time used to make beams and joists. Squared with an adze, the natural curve of the timbers was retained. But saws, which began to be used in the late 17th century, cut timbers straight whatever their natural inclinations.

The treatment of ceilings varied according to region. In some they were whitewashed, in others blackened with walnut stain *(brou de noix),* available in hardware stores today. Plastered ceilings, applied to lath nailed on the underside of joists, became fashionable in the 17th century, but this refinement only recently appeared in farmhouses.

Upstairs flooring. Wide chestnut or poplar planks nailed to the joists were the most popular form of upstairs flooring. But another practice was to lay a bed of *torchis*-dipped sticks across the joists, then cover the sticks with beaten earth. Other floors were 'doubled' by means of wooden strips and the core filled with *torchis,* sand, or even plaster. The upper surface might be planks or sometimes tiles (fig 3).

3. Transverse section of loft floor shows beams, torchis *filling and examples of both tile and plank flooring.*

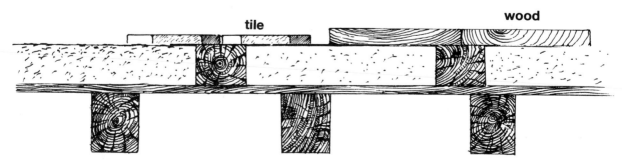

tile **wood**

71

VAULTS

Vaults were common in many parts of France. They roofed wine cellars and supported floors and first floor verandas; but their fullest development was in the Rouergue and Cévennes, where vaults were used to build the entire house.

The most common vault was the **barrel vault,** popular in both Burgundy and Provence. It was erected over a wooden cradle (fig 1) that held the stones in place while the mortar between them set, after which the cradle was dismantled. The disadvantage of barrel vaulting was its considerable lateral thrust, which meant walls had to be very thick.

A more sophisticated solution was the **groined vault** in which two barrel vaults intersect (fig 2), distributing the thrust in four directions. Groined vaults can be seen the Rouergue, Provence and in Savoy.

A third vault, the **corbelled vault**, is more primitive. A circle of stones was laid in rows which overlapped progressively inwards (fig 3). Known since pre-historic times, the dry-stone 'beehive' cabins found throughout Provence, the Causses and Périgord show this technique in its earliest form. Corbelled vaulting bound with mortar sometimes roofed dovecotes and wells but, most commonly, it was used to build bake ovens – and is also called 'oven vaulting'.

2. Groined or intersecting vault.

1. Barrel vault constructed on wood scaffolding.

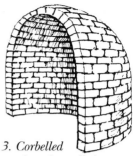

3. Corbelled vaults, also called oven vaults, are the oldest mode of vault construction.

FIREPLACES & CHIMNEYS

The earliest fireplaces were floors. A fire was laid in the centre and the smoke went out through a hole in the roof (fig la), if there was one. Later, a short wattle and daub chimney replaced the hole (fig lb). A developed off-

1. and 2. Fireplace evolution from central hearth to gable chimney.

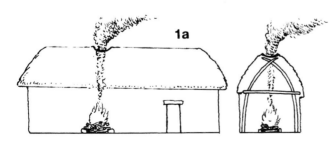

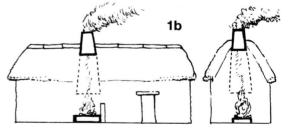

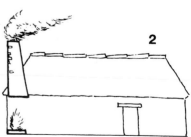

shoot of this arrangement is seen in the mountainous regions of eastern France. Called a *tué,* it is described in detail under Franche-Comté.

The movement of fireplaces from the centre of rooms was due to the development of gable chimneys (fig 2). Installed in seigneurial houses by the 15th century, they appeared in peasant homes two or three hundred years later.

Chimneys revolutionized domestic life. Instead of inhabiting smoke-

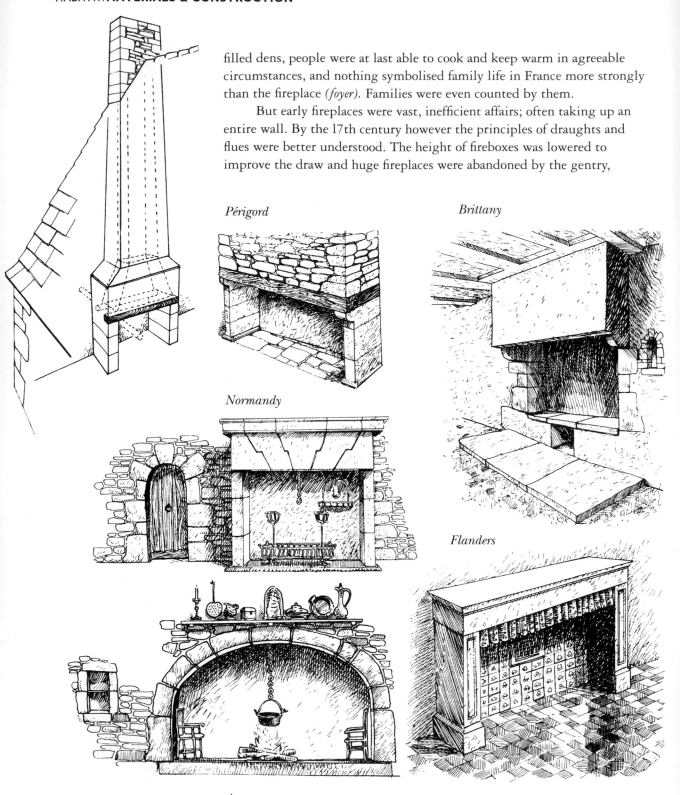

filled dens, people were at last able to cook and keep warm in agreeable circumstances, and nothing symbolised family life in France more strongly than the fireplace *(foyer)*. Families were even counted by them.

But early fireplaces were vast, inefficient affairs; often taking up an entire wall. By the 17th century however the principles of draughts and flues were better understood. The height of fireboxes was lowered to improve the draw and huge fireplaces were abandoned by the gentry,

Périgord

Brittany

Normandy

Flanders

Auvergne

except in kitchens. But they continued in peasant houses, serving as cookers, central heating systems and domestic forums round which the family gathered in the evenings. Festooned with cooking implements, the largest had a settle inside for the elderly and up to the mid-19th century a tinderbox stood beside the hearth. Niches, set into the back wall, were places of safekeeping or, lower down, for collecting the ashes used for washing clothes; and some fireplaces contained a bread oven, though quite often these were separate structures.

Part of regional style, the more imposing fireplaces were built of dressed stone; but most were rubble limestone, the hood supported by a lintel resting on corbels or plinths. All open fireplaces burned wood.

If chimneys smoked or the draught was poor, one solution was to raise the hearth which, in Provence, became the local style. Another solution was to string a frill across the chimney breast, a custom that has not yet disappeared in France.

Chimney stacks (*souches*) were built of rubble or dressed stone or, as in the Vendée, wattle and daub. Some were flush with the wall, some extruded.From the 18th century brick was also used and stone chimneys were sometimes finished in brick above the roof-line in order to save hoisting heavy stones.

Though gables are the most usual position for chimneys, supporting walls were also used. In some places, Flanders for example, a centrally placed chimney helped support the house.

Vendée

Auvergne

Rouergue

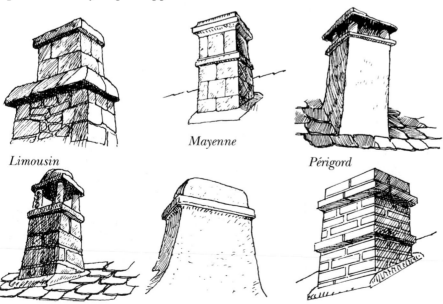

Limousin

Mayenne

Périgord

Guyenne

Alps

Brittany

Normandy

Ile de France

STAIRS

Stone stairs predated wooden ones in France, spiralling romantically up manor house turrets lighted by slit windows. Exterior stone stairs appeared at about the same time in high-houses, the steps parallel or

1. Exterior stone stairs run parallel or at right angles to facades.

perpendicular to the facade (fig 1). But most households used ladders. These gave ready access to lofts but, since hands were not free, what needed storing could not easily be carried up. The solution was a sort of ladder-stair or 'mill ladder', **échelle de meunier** as it was called, probably after its place of origin (fig 2). Mill ladders continued to be used in modest houses through the 19th century. Taking up little space, they were relatively simple to erect.

Conventional staircases were constructed following one of two basic techniques: **à la francaise** in which the steps were encased by boards called *limons* (fig 3) or (less frequently) **à l'anglaise** where treads overhung the supporting frame (fig 4). Banisters were either turned – often in one of the popular Louis XIII patterns – or left plain. Oak and chestnut were the preferred woods and, in more prosperous houses, stair treads might be faced with terracotta.

During the 18th century, enclosed staircases (fig 5) came into vogue. Effective at stopping draughts, they dispensed with complicated banisters, as a hand-rail could be run along the wall. In the 19th century, stairs increasingly occupied a central corridor or vestibule; but in older or simpler houses they stayed put in the kitchen corner – especially *les échelles de meunier.*

2. Mill ladder: the simplest form of fixed stair.

3. Stairs with encased steps: à la francaise.

5. Enclosed stairs were located in kitchen corners or a central corridor.

4. Stairs with overhanging treads à l'anglaise.

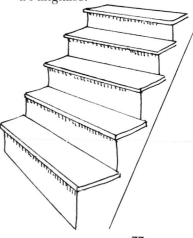

INTERIORS

Though farmhouses look commodious they were rarely so, and attached outbuildings are usually to blame for the deception. Most typically houses comprised only two rooms: a kitchen-cum-living room called the *salle* (or *salle commune)* and a bedroom *(chambre).* But in some regions the *salle* was called *'maison'* (house), a reference to the many centuries during which one room had supplied all needs; and despite the emergence of a second room, this continued in most of France well into the present century. Like hut and medieval hall, the *salle* was the centre of every aspect of domestic life. Families cooked, ate, slept and gathered there. The *chambre* was generally reserved for girls (adolescent sons slept in the barn). It had no fireplace and was sparsely furnished with a bed or two, a wardrobe and perhaps a crucifix or a religious print. But a number of *chambres* were store rooms.

The chief exception to this pervasively two-room plan is found in parts of the south and east where patriarchal family systems prevailed. Sheltering two or three generations, some of these houses are very spacious indeed – nine rooms in Franche-Comté and five or six in the Landes and *pays* Basque. But in all of them the *salle* retained its pre-eminence.

Normally the front door opened directly into the *salle* or, by the late 19th century, perhaps a corridor which divided the two rooms. Decoration consisted of limewashed walls in white or, less often, vivid cerulean blue. The exposed ceiling timbers were either left bare, occasionally painted white or were sometimes artificially darkened with walnut oil – or smoke. There was of course no lavatory nor any outhouse: women resorted to the stable and men to the adjacent fields.

Floors, generally beaten earth before the 19th century, were hosts to pigs and chickens and rubbish was thrown into the centre of the room for their collection. But clay tiles, cheaply produced in the 19th century, transformed this rather crude aspect of life and, though pervious to damp, were a great improvement to health and sanitation. Brick and stone flags were also used for flooring in some regions, *e.g.* Normandy and Burgundy respectively; and occasionally wood.

But the focal point of every household was its fireplace. Fitted with pot hooks and a crane; a trivet, cooking pots and kettle were ranged along the hearth and in front of it, throne-like, stood the master's seat. Sometimes a settle was placed inside the fireplace for the elderly, while a cloth frill, intended to help the chimney draw, gave the room its only –

Landaise salle *with traditional furnishings.*

Simply-draped 'Empire' style bed.

and misleading – hint of frivolity.

The *salle's* other permanent fixture was a sink *(évier)*. This was a shallow stone trough embedded in a niche in the wall. A shelf was often installed above the sink and outdoors the drain pipe was extended by a protruding, grooved stone that conducted water away from the foundations (see page 147).

Beside the fireplace (or under a window) it was customary to find a *potager,* a sort of brazier on legs where slow cooking over charcoal was done. Normally built of masonry, a grill was set in the top and embers from the fireplace put into the cavity beneath.

Embedded stone sink: a fixture in every household.

From the mid-18th century peasant families began slowly to increase their personal belongings, so that by the late 19th century the *salle* was becoming rather crowded. It contained beds, a cradle, a table and benches and a fireside seat, plus one or more wardrobes, a dresser and/or a cabinet. A tendency towards specialization resulted in the appearance of a dough trough, salt box, spoon and bread racks and, in wealthier houses, a number of useful trifles like bulbous glass flycatchers, bonnet cabinets and wooden walkways for toddlers. Pots and pans had multiplied around the fireplace and religious prints – or even a photograph – hung over the mantelpiece. Special ceramic jars for storing *confit,* oil, etc also came into fashion; while against the *salle* wall a longcase clock ticked steadily, chiming the hours and half hours (twice) and putting church bells out of business as the established authorities of worldly time.

FURNITURE

Surprisingly, country furniture was roughly the same all over France; but its detail differed significantly. As with architecture there evolved in each province a vernacular style based on local skills, predilections and available woods. But overall innovation seeped slowly down from the Court and, once adopted by a locale, rarely changed again. Susceptible to improvements, peasants could not afford the ephemerality of fashion.

The reigns of the Bourbon kings Louis XIII to Louis XVI (1610 to 1789) saw the development of France's *'grands styles'* of furniture-making. Admired throughout the western world, two of these styles had a seminal impact on French country furniture: Louis XIII and Louis XV; and furniture from these periods continued to be made in rural workshops through the 19th century, often with a touch of other 'Louis' styles mixed in.

Louis XV-style panel.

'Louis XIII' is a linear, somewhat architectural style with massive proportions, elaborately turned posts and balusters and sombrely carved geometric decoration – principally diamonds and discs. It was still being made in more conservative regions, *e.g.* Brittany, Guyenne and Gascony, nearly 300 years after Louis XIII's death.

'Louis XV', which became much more pervasive, is altogether different: lighter in appearance with fluid curves and graceful, human proportions, its decoration is drawn from nature and abounds with delicate floral relief.

Country craftsmen interpreted France's 'grand styles' with varying degrees of naivety or refinement and it is their unselfconscious, sometimes quite primitive rendering that brings a special beauty and verve to the furniture they produced. Moreover peasant parsimony appears to have yielded in this area to a yen for ornamentation, as decoration was repeatedly indulged in even on the most primitive pieces.

The wood for country furniture came mainly from local forests: oak, chestnut, walnut and beech being the most desirable. But fruitwood, especially cherry, was preferred for carving the graceful contours of Louis XV pieces: usually it was wild cherry since cutting down an orchard tree would have been thought lunatic.

In mountainous areas, where softwoods were the only option, furniture was quite often painted.

BEDS Rural French beds were usually four feet wide and had at least two occupants. The mattress was made of straw or leaves in very poor houses; wool or feathers in better-off ones. The sheets and blankets were woven at home and a plump feather quilt *(couette)* and bolster completed the bedding.

Breton box bed.

Bed à la duchesse.

In such crowded surroundings privacy was as desirable as warmth, so beds were hung with curtains or boxed in wooden frames. Affording a tent-like privacy (occupants dressed and undressed inside), bed hangings also kept out insects and dust.

Beds were usually placed in corners, against a wall or in an alcove; which is why they are often more plainly finished on one side than the other. Four types of bed were common.

Box beds *(lits-clos)* were, as the name suggests, totally enclosed by wooden panels (Brittany) or were semi-boxed and hung with curtains (Normandy, Auvergne, Savoy). Standing in corners at right angles to the fire or ranged along the wall like panelling, their often high legs left plenty of storage space below and also kept the occupants safe from rising damp. In parts of the Alps, sheep slept underneath as bedwarmers.

Quite often, especially in Brittany, a chest was placed beside the bed to make a step, exactly as in Italian Renaissance frescoes – and it could double as a seat at dinner.

Two-and four posted beds *(lits à quenouilles)* had canopies that were either attached to the bed posts or suspended from the ceiling.

Charente, Touraine, Burgundy, Bresse and Alsace all favoured such beds. Often elegantly draped, those with full canopies and the bedstead entirely concealed by fabric were called *à la duchesse*.

Angel beds *(lits d'ange)*, popular in the south, were made of four short posts with a plain headboard and no foot board. The absence of a foot board is said to have made this an excellent bed for delivering babies. Angel bed canopies were, like half testers, always shorter than the bed's length. A similar bed but without hangings and called a *litoche* was ubiquitous in Provence.

'Empire' beds. In the late 19th century, a country version of Empire-style beds, with head and foot boards the same height, became popular, either hung with a length of fabric draped over a rod *(lit à flèche)* or with hangings suspended from a coronet *(lit en pavillon)*.

Provençal litoche.

CHESTS *(coffres).* The wonder of the wheel is remarked upon in schoolrooms everywhere but the box's invention has been taken for granted. As the earliest furniture, boxes – or chests – proved enormously useful. Repositories for clothes, household linens and valuable papers if they existed, chests also made excellent grain stores since rodents could not get in. Specially carved and decorated they became marriage chests. They also performed the functions of bedsteps, benches, money boxes, trunks and tables, and were the antecedents of much other furniture as will be seen.

Early chest from Champagne.

WARDROBES (*armoires*) to many minds epitomize French provincial furniture. First appearing in farmhouses in the 18th century their popularity was such that they rapidly displaced the use of chests in most of France. The wardrobe's shelves made storage and retrieval of clothes and linens far easier than rummaging in chests. Moreover wardrobes had considerable social cachet, most in evidence as the essential item of a bride's trousseau. In this instance their size and decoration were important indexes of family wealth and, in Normandy, where their highest refinement was achieved, buying one was a great occasion.

The bride's family and the engaged couple visited the cabinetmaker where they were given dinner, after which the cabinetmaker presented his models. The price depended largely on the amount of decoration – the number of roses being the principal key. Finally, on the wedding eve the trousseau-laden wardrobe was ceremoniously delivered to the groom's house in a cart, accompanied by violins.

TABLES (*tables*) were usually placed in the centre of the *salle* or under a window. For centuries they were removable boards on trestles – highly suitable when space was dear. For this reason too fixed-leg tables often had dual roles, with deep drawers or a chest underneath for storing food or milk. Flanking benches formed the seating and some tables had sliding panels instead of drawers so that they could be opened without inconvenience to the sitters. Many tables could be enlarged for special occasions by hooking a plank on each end or placing one over the pulled out end drawers. The table was then covered with a cloth.

A round drop-leaf table was another space saver. Called a wine table in Burgundy and Champagne it was also popular in Picardy farmhouses, where some charming examples are found.

CABINETS (*buffets*) are really chests that open in front, which means things could be conveniently stored on top. Most cabinets had two doors and a drawer or two but in Picardy, Artois and Flanders they were of great length, having up to eight doors, and a shelf hanging above the cabinet for pots. A Provençal variation, the *buffet à gradin,* was topped by a tiny two-drawer cabinet attached to the main cabinet body.

Chest-on-chests (*bahuts*) were more typical of bourgeois homes.

Opposite, left to right: Norman wardrobe, Breton dresser with clock built in, wine table and Provençal buffet à gradin.

DRESSERS (*vaisseliers*) began to appear in farmhouses with the spread of earthenware dishes. Combining a chest, drawers and display shelves their importance varied from province to province: central to Lorraine households for instance they were unknown in Flanders or Picardy where other solutions (see above) developed.

Some dressers have a gallery fronting the shelves, which occasionally included a spoon rack; and a few dressers, *e.g.* in Bresse, have a clock built into the centre of the shelves. Though two doors was the norm, three or more was not uncommon and in lower Normandy the cabinet section was replaced by open shelves for pails (though some models have a cabinet *above* the shelves).

Right: baluster-studded food safe from Champagne and Basque settle or zuzulu.

Below: grandfather clock from the Franche-Comté.

SAFES *(garde-manger)*. Food was generally stored in specially-built safes or in cupboards embedded in the wall, the doors being either pierced or inlaid with balusters for ventilation. Bread usually had a separate store. In Provence this was a wooden cage always hung, despite its having short legs, above the dough trough. Elsewhere a bread shelf hung from the ceiling over the table or a slotted rack was used.

SEATS *(sièges)* were either benches, settles or a straw-bottomed chair placed beside the fire. Bretons for example favoured a baluster-backed bench or a settle with a chest beneath while the Basques invented a special settle, the *zuzulu*. Able to seat three the *zuzulu* was reserved for the master and those he wished to join him, but the centre panel folded neatly forward to make a little table between two seats.

A small frame-back chair was also seen in farmhouses and, in the west, a 'salt seat'. This bench-cum-chest had a flap in the middle of the seat and was said to have been invented for hiding salt during the despised salt tax – by sitting on it.

CLOCKS *(horloges)*. By the late 19th century most households had a longcase clock, its enamel dial framed by a sumptuous pressed brass surround depicting a scene. The clock's pendulum was either totally exposed inside the case – and therefore decorated – or only the disc on the end showed through a circular window.

Though clocks were made in many regions, Franche-Comté was the centre of the craft and provided welcome winter employment for the snowed-in peasants. Franche-Comté clocks were shipped all over France but their cases as a rule were locally made, conforming therefore to traditional regional style.

Clock cases had a number of shapes: straight, pyramidal, violin-shaped and, in Normandy where the lower half curved like a woman's hips – *demoiselle*. Though pine and fir were popular woods for cases and relatively inexpensive, cherry, oak and walnut were much used and a number of clock cases were painted.

CRADLES *(berceaux),* part of every household, had either knobs or holes on the sides for lacing the baby in and many cradles had stands in order to place the baby above the reach of animals; alternatively a table or chair was used. In Bresse however the cradle was hooked between the end posts of the bed and could be rocked by the foot without getting up.

DOUGH TROUGHS *(pétrins)* varied from simple scooped out troughs (Corrèze) to elegantly carved boxes set on legs (Provence). Designed for kneading dough many became general storage chests.

DRAINING BOARDS *(égouttoirs)* were slatted crates on legs that enabled dishes to be drip-dried, and several had one or more shelves for dry storage on top.

LIGHTING There was little lighting in peasant homes. Few could read and firelight often sufficed for evening knitting and spinning or repairs. Before kerosene lamps became widely available at the turn of the century however oil- or fat-burning lamps were kept on hand; also tallow candles and, for very special occasions, beeswax.

Long cradle legs were protection against domestic animals.

Draining board for drip-drying dishes and dough trough or pétrin.

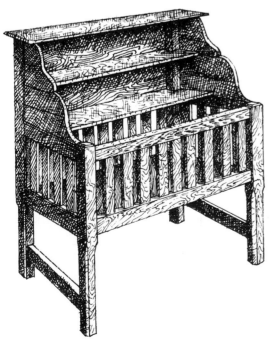

OUTBUILDINGS

Outbuildings, as has been pointed out, were an integral part of every farmhouse; reflecting the mode of farming which, for most of France, was subsistence crops or, on very poor or hilly land, agro-pastoral farming – usually sheep or goats.

A stable, barn and (where needed) sheepfold were standard annexes; if geography permitted there was a well. But by the mid-19th century, as the economy improved, separate lodgings for pigs and chickens became common and many farms had bake ovens. In addition special buildings were constructed for particular activities: cider and wine-making, silkworm nurture, drying hemp and of course rearing pigeons. All were built in the local style, blending harmoniously with the architecture of the house.

GRANARIES & BARNS

Crop storage was essential and the lofts of houses normally served as a granary (*grenier*). Steeply pitched roofs provided copious storage space and admitted dormers and smaller openings (*houteaux*) so that crops could be hoisted into the loft, and then ventilated. But where the roof slope was weak, leaving little room beneath, *i.e.* canal-tiled roofs, walls were often raised to make a half-storey that became the granary, aired by small unglazed windows in the facade.

By the 19th century most farms also had a barn (*grange*). Barns were multi-functional: serving as combination granaries, haylofts (*fenils*) and straw stores (*paillers*) they also contained a cart shed approached by huge double doors, and sometimes a threshing floor. Many older barns also housed pigs, chickens and rabbits. Others, blurring into a stable, contained a cowshed.

Most but not all barns were constructed in the same material as the house, and some of them are enormous. They were ventilated by small windows (*jours*) or by gaps between wooden planks, as in the Alps and Vosges. A number had owl holes under the gables so that the birds could act rat catcher.

The most spectacular barns of all are on the northern plains, especially Champagne, Brie, the Beauce and Soissonnais. The oldest were attached to abbeys or monasteries and usually have very low walls, the roof weight resting on interior posts (see Aisled hall construction), since weight-

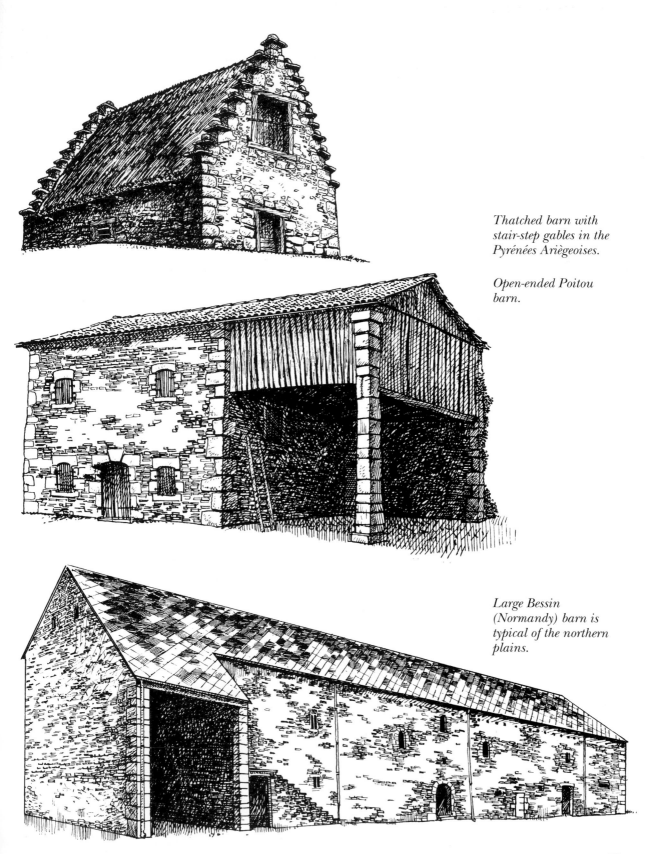

*Thatched barn with
stair-step gables in the
Pyrénées Ariègeoises.*

*Open-ended Poitou
barn.*

*Large Bessin
(Normandy) barn is
typical of the northern
plains.*

carrying walls had not yet been fully developed. But though some big barns date from the 15th and 16th centuries the majority are 18th and 19th century and were built, following the development of artificial prairies, to store cereals.

In milder climates – Poitou and the Garonne valley for example – open hangars or Dutch barns were common, attached to the house or separate, the roof supported by stone or brick pillars.

But not all barns are separate buildings. In the Alps, Franche Comté and Vosges the barn occupied the entire loft of what are often vast dwellings; a hillside ramp admitted hay wagons to the upper level, and some lofts contained a threshing floor.

STABLES

Most peasants owned one or two cows and these were family treasures. In addition to milk and butter cows produced valuable manure – and calves, which were normally sold because of insufficient pasture.

On small farms the cow was tethered in a stable (*étable*) contiguous with the house. Milked twice a day – women's work – it was minded in the pasture by a child.

On larger, agro-pastoral farms accommodation for a herd was needed and a successful answer was the *grange-étable*. This combination barn-stable housed both animals and fodder. The lower level was the cow house, with mangers along one or both sides and drainage in the centre aisle. Hay was taken into the loft by means of a ramp and could then be forked directly into the mangers below. Originally thatched, *granges-étables* were later covered with *lauzes* or slates (see also Limousin and Auvergne).

Where horses were kept stalls were necessary. Called an *écurie*, the word is often interchangeable with *étable*. Proper *écuries* were rare in the south since oxen not horses were used for ploughing. (Horses ploughed faster but they ate more – and needed oats, which could not be slotted into the south's two-field rotation system.)

It was common practice in France for sons and hired men to sleep in the stable (or barn). A corner was kitted out with a bed or else the men slept on the straw. Able to keep a close eye on the animals the practice also had its social uses given the intimacy of sleeping quarters in the house.

In the Alps families and sometimes whole villages regularly gathered in the stable on winter evenings. Mending tools and doing needlework they gossiped and told each other tales, kept warm by their animals' body heat. These gatherings, called *veillées*, are much celebrated in accounts of peasant life and the art of storytelling appears to have been highly developed.

Bedroom kitted out in corner of stable for son or hired hand.

Early Champagne Berrichon barn roofed in slates, flat tiles and modern mechanical tiles.

SHEEPFOLDS

Sheepfolds (*bergeries*) were long, low buildings with movable hurdle fencing inside so that rams and mothers with lambs could be separated as needed. Often located at a distance from the house some 19th century sheepfolds sheltered up to 1000 sheep or goats, though one or two hundred animals was more usual. On very smallholdings however the sheep were often lodged in part of the barn.

Sheepfolds were for wintering. In summer flocks were pastured, and the lush meadows of the Alps, Pyrénées and Massif Central caused animal husbandry to flourish in the surrounding areas. In May the flocks were driven along ancient paths or *drailles* up to the high pastures, sometimes as communal herds and sometimes under the aegis of a family herdsman. The shepherds lodged in small cabins with cheese making facilities attached. (On the plains they often lived in huts on wheels). When the pastures were far away, progress was made in stages and a string of small barns stocked with fodder helped to sustain the animals en route (see also Alps).

Until the 20th century each region had its own breed, developed over centuries to suit that particular environment (just as the local architecture developed); but this changed with the introduction of selective breeding methods.

Another result of improved agriculture was that where artificial prairies appeared, sheep gave way to cattle. Cattle were much more valuable. But though flocks dwindled in the Landes and Beauce for instance they continued as before in many mountain areas and, on the plain of Larzac, greatly multiplied to meet the demands of an expanding Roquefort cheese industry. Larzac sheepfolds have a particular character: stone-built, their roofs are constructed in a pointed arch, making the long buildings look like squat cathedrals.

Goats also survived thanks to the cheese industry and today France's prime goat breeding region is Poitou.

Pebble-built sheepfold in the Camargue (Provence).

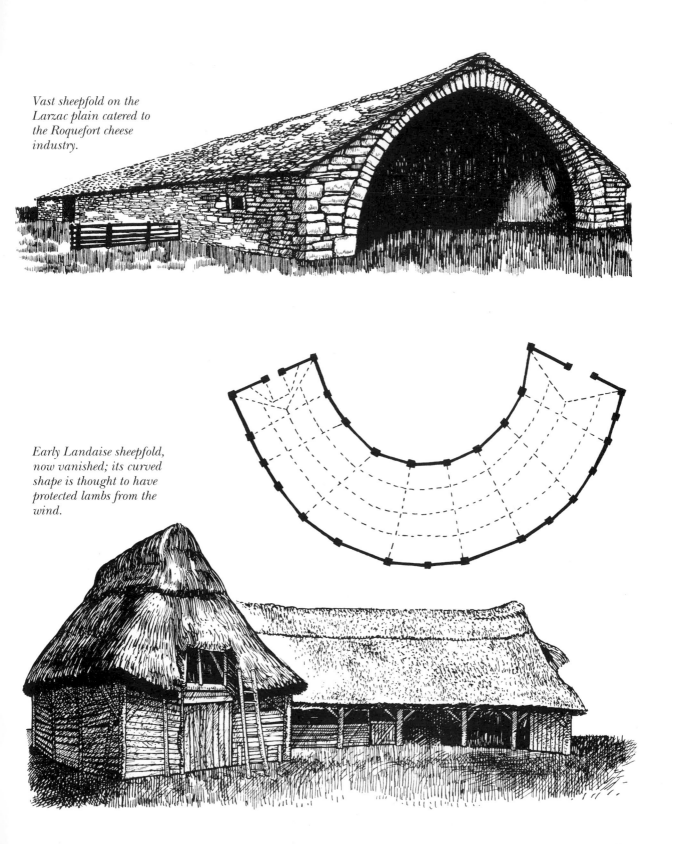

Vast sheepfold on the Larzac plain catered to the Roquefort cheese industry.

Early Landaise sheepfold, now vanished; its curved shape is thought to have protected lambs from the wind.

SMALL OUTBUILDINGS

Chickenhouses, piggeries and rabbit hutches proliferated on late 19th century farms, suggesting an improved economy and possibly an interest in new ideas about farming.

For centuries pigs had run loose, living on acorns in the forest, or were haphazardly penned up in a corner of the barn. Remnants of circular pigstys exist in Brittany but by the 19th century pig houses generally consisted of a row of cubicles, each with a stone trough that could be filled from outside. Normally constructed of stone the building was about the height of a man and the roof quite often was one-sloped.

Barnyard fowl foraged in a similiar way to pigs, scratching out a living in the yard, wandering into the house at will and pecking scraps off the earthen floor. But they needed housing to protect them at night from vermin. Roosting in the barn was one solution but a combination pig-and-chickenhouse – the chicken coop occupying the upper storey – was more elegant. Many of these were constructed with great care, attached or separate from the house itself; and a number, as in Berry, were built against the gable and next to the oven vault where it was warm.

Unusual lattice-work chickenhouse with pigsty beneath.

But the most ingenious chickenhouse of all is in the Landes. Vermin were a special menace in the forest and so chicken houses were put on stilts. Rectangular wooden huts with tiled roofs, a ladder or notched pole allowed the birds to mount and a slatted floor permitted their precious droppings to be saved for fertilizer.

Poultry were looked after by women but neither chickens nor eggs were eaten at home. To eat a chicken would have been devouring capital – something no thrifty housewife would have dreamt of. As for the eggs, they went to market and egg money was often the only cash a peasant family earned.

Rabbit has always been a favourite on French dinner tables and most 19th century farms kept a hutch (*clapier*) in the barn – usually wire-fronted cages where animals were bred and reared for sale.

*Left: Landaise
chickenhouse on stilts,
with balancing well in
background.*

*A Breton pigsty lovingly
preserved.*

WELLS & CISTERNS

On every farm livestock had to be watered and clothes and dishes washed; though bodies apparently did not. But given the constant need for water, a nearby river proved a godsend and a spring bubbling out of the ground, miraculous. In fact the word for spring, *source*, is the root of 'sorcerer' – originally a water diviner – and it is easy to understand the reverence in which such persons were held: most farmers had to dig a well, an arduous business and not always a successful one; divine assistance must have seemed a colossal boon.

Water tends to be plentiful in impermeable soils and farmsteads could have their own wells, and so disperse; but water in permeable soils is not so forthcoming, causing farmers to band together and build their houses round a communal well. Where the soil was too porous to hold any water however – as on the limestone *causses* – cisterns were necessary and to this end tree trunks were split, hollowed out and put under the eaves, making a network of primitive guttering that drained into a tank.

Communal wells were located sensibly in the village square but on dispersed farms they normally stood in front of the house, near the kitchen. Drawing water was women's work and in a day several trips might be necessary to keep a full bucket beside the kitchen sink.

It is probably due to water's scarcity – and the difficulty of getting it – that clothes and household linens were washed only twice a year, in spring and autumn. This great biannual washing took three days to complete.

Two main types of wells were dug: the most common, a cylinder normally lined with stones, and balancing wells. Balancing wells are very shallow and a pole with a bucket on one end was ducked and levered up seesaw-like to draw the water. Balancing wells are frequent in North Africa and their presence in France may be a legacy from the Moors, pushed back across the Pyrénées by Charles Martel in the eighth century. Generally such wells contain brackish water and are extremely unhealthy. But this was true of most drinking water, and wine's reputedly tonic value may stem from the fact that those who drank it instead of water stayed healthier.

The most usual means of drawing water was with a rope wound on a roller, or by a pulley system. Only at the end of the 19th century did hand pumps come into use and then they were rare indoors.

The design of wellheads (*margelles*) and wellhousing accorded very much to local style and ranged from simple square or round wellheads

The biannual wash. First water was boiled and poured over the clothes. A bag of wood ash placed in the cauldron helped to clean them by releasing salts. The water was then siphoned off and reheated, and the process repeated several times. Finally the clothes were beaten and rinsed. In villages this last stage occurred at the washhouse, a sort of shed beside a shallow pool, and a sacred preserve of women.

(Périgord) to near monumental structures of carved stone (Brittany). A beehive-shape, a variation on earlier dry-stone constructions, is typical of several regions and, in parts of western France, a niche for the Virgin or a local saint was included, hinting at older purification rituals – for if water cleansed bodies it was reasoned, would it not do the same for souls?

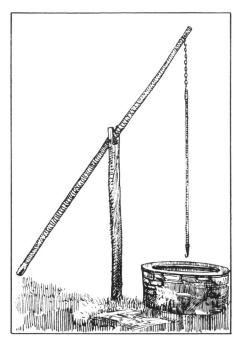

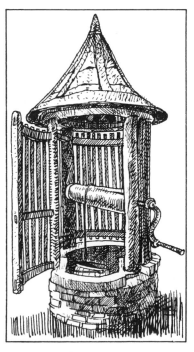

Four styles of well: balancing well, beehive well developed from dry-stone hut construction, carved Breton well and a Normandy well protected by slat casing.

BAKEHOUSES & OVENS

As bread was the staple food bake ovens had primal importance – something seigneurs were quick to turn to their advantage. They built communal ovens (*fours banals*) and, charging the peasants to use them, forbade them to build their own. It was the same with milling: to grind corn peasants were forced to use the lord's mill, and to pay for it with part of the flour. At every stage of bread-making therefore the lord profited, having already taken part of the harvest.

By the 17th century however many villages, and later on individuals, began to build their own ovens and these were of two types: *four* (oven) and *fournil* (bakehouse).

FOUR The dome-shaped oven or *four* consists of a corbelled brick vault, usually with a cast iron door. The convex shape plus the porosity of the brick helped to create an even temperature throughout. A casing of stone, *pisé* or turf completed the insulation. The oven was either attached to the house, sharing the fireplace flue, or it was built free-standing without a flue. Some free-standing ovens were protected by a shed-like roof that also kept the woodpile dry.

FOURNIL A bakehouse or *fournil* is a small rectangular building with its own chimney and enough space in front of the oven to bake protected from the weather. Though many bakehouses were communal their use on farms depended on regional preference more than wealth. But separation

Communal bakehouse on tiny village green in the Auvergne.

of bakehouse and dwelling greatly reduced the risk of fire in thatched and half-timbered regions – at one time over half the country.

Baking was a complex business and it was never a daily one, occurring once a week or every ten days and in some alpine regions only twice a year.

First a bundle of lit faggots was put into the oven and pushed progressively towards the back with a poker. The smoke went out through the open oven door and up the chimney in front of it, if there was one. Stoking continued till the vault turned grey, at which point the door was closed briefly to allow the heat to spread; then the ashes were removed and

Sheltered oven in the Landes with ample space for woodpile. Bottom: turf covered Breton oven and a canal-tiled variation.

the oven floor mopped clean.

The dough was put in the oven with a long paddle and baking it took about an hour. Afterwards pastries and cakes, which required a lower temperature, were baked.

Emilie Carles' vivid memoir of alpine life* describes pre-winter baking in local villages before World War I. The peasants brought their own wood and drew lots to see who would start the oven and go first, this being the trickiest moment: there was no sure way to check the oven temperature and what they were baking had to sustain them all winter.

The fresh-baked loaves were then wrapped in cloth and stored in safes or on shelves suspended from the ceiling. In Emilie Carles' village the shelves hung in the barn and the bread, taken down as needed during the winter, was suspended over the sheep pen to soften. Even then only a special knife could cut it and pieces would fly across the room. But the bread was reputedly delicious: the thick crusts encasing each loaf like a carapace made good insulators. Moreover white (wheat) bread, which is quick to lose its freshness, was never peasant fare; it was generally rye (black), though buckwheat and several mixed grains were common too.

PLUMS AND CHESTNUTS Some bakehouses were specially adapted for drying plums or chestnuts. The latter, known as a *clédier*, was typical of Limousin and the Cévennes, where chestnuts formed the peasants' daily bread. Built like ordinary bakehouses *clédiers* have slatted ceilings. Chestnuts were spread over the slats and dried by heat from the open oven or by fires lit on the bakehouse floor.

Plum or prune ovens, common in the Garonne valley, were quite often attached to the gable entrance of barns where they look like small bakehouses. Their job was to partially dry plums placed on racks that pivoted from a central post, enabling the exposure to vary and the fruit itself to be turned.

HEMP Though the process was similar to that of drying chestnuts, a different oven architecture was required for drying hemp. Found in Maine for example the oven looks like a squat dovecote with two entrances, one above the other. The lower level housed a firebasket and the upper level, approached by stone steps, contained the bundles of hemp – the levels being divided by a slatted floor. It seems unlikely that workers exhuming the dried hemp from its smoky chamber would have missed the headier pleasures of this crop which, as marijuana, mesmerized so many smokers in the 1960s.

* A Wild Herb Soup

DOVECOTES

The Roman practice of rearing pigeons in dovecotes was revived in France at the beginning of the Middle Ages. The earliest extant dovecotes (*pigeonniers*) are however round towers dating from the 16th century. Towers have always been synonymous with the grander aspects of French architecture, adding elegance and prestige to any property that possessed one; but in the case of pigeons it was economic more than social gain that made such structures so desirable.

Pigeons are comparatively easy to raise; they breed rapidly, produce eggs and make good eating. Nor do housed birds need shooting – a boon to peasants who before the Revolution were forbidden to hunt. But most important of all pigeons produced excellent fertilizer and in areas where livestock was scarce, as in Quercy, this factor more than any other triggered the proliferation of dovecotes in the countryside. In fact pigeon fertilizer is so rich it had to be diluted and the precious droppings were often bequeathed in wills.

The drawback to pigeon rearing was that although birds fed themselves what they ate often belonged to others – and in a year two pigeons could consume a hundred pounds of grain. The anger and frustration felt by those on whose land the birds fattened led in the 16th century to restrictions on rearing them. Throughout most of the north dovecotes became the exclusive right of seigneurs, presumably because they were large landowners; but this cannot have made life any easier for their tenants. In the south the solution was more democratic, pigeon numbers being limited by property size. Local custom varied: one nest per acre of land has been recorded but the ratio must have run higher in many places given the number of dovecotes: by the 18th century there were more than 42,000 of them, constructed of stone, half-timbering or a decorative pattern work of brick, stone and flint.

But complaints of crop damage continued and during the Revolution peasants demanded a law keeping pigeons shut up in July and August to protect the harvest. In the north, where complaints were especially strong, a number of dovecotes, by now hated symbols of class oppression, shared the fate of many a chateau tower and were pulled down.

Of round or square construction (a few are hexagonal) the overall plan of dovecotes is of two kinds: *à pied* refers to standing towers with nests from top to bottom. Usually part of large estates these dovecotes housed between one and three thousand nests. The chateau of Hagrou à Maule in the Yvelines had 3200 nests and six people were attached to its service.

But the style most typical of smaller properties and found throughout the south had only the upper half reserved for birds; the lower

*Opposite page,
left to right:
bullet-shaped dovecote
from the Gers; two
seigneurial Norman
dovecotes – brick and
chalk, from Caux and
thatch, stone and
pebbles in the Marais
Vernier; the one-sloped* à
casquette *style is
typical of the south.*

*Dovecote mounted on
pillars dominates
Agenais (Guyenne)
landscape.*

part was used to store grain or tools and sometimes house chickens or pigs. A modification of this type rested gracefully on pillars or arches or perched impressively on the top of houses and barns.

In older and grander dovecotes the nesting quarters were built into the masonry, the thick walls becoming a sort of petrified honeycomb. A ladder attached to a central pivot enabled nests to be serviced. In smaller dovecotes baskets or pottery nailed to the walls was used for nesting.

Openings to admit the birds were usually in the form of dormers or a cupola and a small ledge was necessary for take-off and landing. The openings were sized to keep out larger birds.

Other devices protected pigeons from vermin. A masonry collar encircled free-standing dovecotes while a slippery surface of glazed tiles or zinc sometimes surrounded entrance holes. Dovecotes set on pillars were protected by mushroom-like capitals to stop predators climbing up.

The steep roofs, usually conical or pavilion style, were covered with local materials. But in the south a slanted one-sloped roof (*à casquette or pied de mulet*) designed to protect birds from the prevailing wind was popular from the Garonne valley to Provence. Pottery pigeons on the roof encouraged the birds to land.

Restrictions on dovecotes were lifted during the Revolution and by the mid-19th century even the smallest farmhouse had pigeonholes under the roof, especially in the south. Peasants could now produce food and fertilizer in a few square metres of space, making dovecotes one the earliest instances of intensive farming. (And unlike those which followed, it suited the gregarious nature of this species.)

The arrival of chemical fertilizers more than any other factor brought the tradition of dovecotes to an end. Today pigeon-rearing is largely the hobby of pigeon fanciers, notably in the Pas de Calais; and dovecotes, among the most charming of France's domestic architectural features, have reverted to their secondary use – prestige, to which has been added a considerable dollop of romance.

WINE CELLARS

The architectural requirements for wine-making were two rooms with a constant and coolish temperature — one or both of them dark: the *cuvier* (sometimes improvised) where wine was made and the store room for maturing it in casks and bottles, called a *chai*, *cave* or *cellier* depending on the region. (In Champagne the *cuvier* is called a *cellier*.)

Chais, prevalent in the south are ground floor cellars usually located on the north side of houses. But in northern France where heavy frosts occur wine was stored underground in dug *caves*, semi-dug versions of which were popular in many regions, including Provence. Underground cellars were usually vaulted either with cradle or intersecting arches. In the Loire valley however natural caves and stone quarries along the river bank became wine stores.

As previously pointed out, high-houses were particularly well-suited to wine-growing in relatively mild climates, their slightly humid ground floors readily accommodating vats and barrels. Where wine was produced on a large scale, as in Languedoc and parts of Provence, the *chais* and *cuviers* were vast rectangular buildings with small demi-lune windows, forming part of the enclosed courtyard of farmsteads.

Peasant wine-growers were usually small freeholders or sharecroppers working for bourgeois landowners. But because of wine's profitability they were generally better off than local farmers, even though their vineyards might be tiny. Wine-growing was enormously labour intensive. Vines had to be fertilized, weeded, ploughed, replaced, pruned, tied up, sprayed and the grapes hand-picked — in addition to the wine-making; but even one hectare produced a lot of wine, most of it swiftly consumed as it did not keep well. For though wine-making was roughly the same as in wine chateaux the art of vinification and type of soil and grapes were usually of inferior quality.

Wine-making. Immediately after picking, grapes were trodden in stone or wooden troughs by bare feet amid much merrymaking; the juice or 'must' running off into a wooden vat or *cuve*. White wine was fermented at once but red wine required maceration of the juice with the crushed skins so the wine could take on their colour. The stems were detached by stirring the grapes with a three-pronged stick and later on the stems rose, together with other debris, to the top of the vat, forming what was called the 'hat'.

When removed from the vat, the skins were pressed by a hydraulic press and the juice either mixed with the new wine or, more often, bottled separately as inferior stock. The last pressing, mixed with water, made *piquette* which the peasants usually drank themselves.

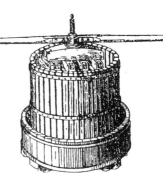

Wine press for pressing grape-skins.

Grape stems were detached by stirring with three-pronged stick.

Fermentation took some six to ten days on average in wooden vats that had been treated with sulphur to remove impurities.

Small particles or 'lees' were removed by 'racking': siphoning the wine through a spout above the settled lees and transferring it to another cask. This normally happened several times in the course of two or three years, depending on the wine. 'Fining' was an additional means of clarification using egg white, ox blood, milk etc which, acting as a magnet, attracted tiny particles in the wine.

After two or three years in casks, and sometimes less, wine was either bottled or sold in the cask.

CIDER MILLS

Before World War I cider was far more usual in peasant homes than wine. But though made on farms everywhere it is chiefly associated with Normandy, where it became a considerable industry. (Cider-making apples

Cider apples were crushed in a stone trough.

are thought to have been introduced into Normandy via Spain after the Hundred Years War.)

First the apples were crushed by an upended millstone trundled by an ox or horse round a circular tub. The millstone was made of wood and the tub it travelled in looked like a gigantic aspic mould. After being crushed the apples were macerated in a vat for eight hours before they were pressed.

The press was a gigantic structure. Descended from ancient Greek presses it was known as a 'long arm' press because of its shaft, on the end of which was a huge wooden screw.

To press the macerated apples ten layers of them were stacked beneath the arm, each layer separated by a bed of straw. Buckwheat straw was said to give the best taste. Then the press was screwed down and the multi-layered sandwich of apples mashed, the juice flowing out through a spout in the base and into chestnut barrels.

After this the pulp was sprinkled with water and a second and third pressing ensued. These last two made '*cidre mitoyen*' or '*petit bère*' which, having less alcohol when fermented, was the daily drink of men at work. (Calvados was made by distilling the cider.)

A rectangular building was required to house the crusher and press with an alcove for the press's long arm. Apples were stored in the loft. Buildings like this are still seen in Normandy but the press is rarely inside them and the trough for crushing apples has, as often as not, been transformed into a doughnut-shaped flowerpot on the lawn.

Long arm press squeezed the juice from the apples.

PEASANT LIFE

On the day he married, Pierre-Alain Hélias walked to his bride's house carrying on his head 24 hemp shirts. The hemp was home-grown and the thread had been spun by his mother. Twenty-four shirts may seem excessive for a young man with little else to his name but the custom of washing clothes twice a year explains it.

Pierre-Alain was rising in the world. He was one of eight children brought up in one room with a mud floor. His bride's house had a mud floor too but there were two rooms, and a cubicle in the attic, which was let. There was a stable and even a lavatory — three boards over a vat. And the house's only other occupant was the bride's father, who owned it himself.

Pierre-Alain Hélias was married in 1913 and the war that was to crack the hardened crust of peasant life was one year off. His son grew up to see their native Brittany transformed from a backward and impoverished land, little changed over centuries, into France's most productive agricultural region. In his famous memoir of Breton village life, 'The Horse of Pride', he captures with great affection that world which after centuries, fixed as in a firmament, imploded and was no more.

Few peasant voices from the past have been heard in France but in them a sombre undertone of hardship, exploitation and brutality is mixed with the philosophic acceptance of survivors: 'I have had the misfortune this year to lose two bullocks and my mule, not to mention Jeanne, my woman, who died at the beginning of the season,' a Berry peasant wrote laconically, his priorities not unusual in a world where food was what life was about.

Outsider accounts of traditional peasant life — Balzac, Pagnol, even the reforming Zola — cannot dismiss the greedy, self-serving and conniving aspects of peasant temperament. And doubtless these were there. Peasant life was indeed nasty, brutish and short and peasants reacted accordingly. The average male lifespan in 1900 was forty-six and from early childhood existence was full of toil, hunger, deprivation and incessant fear: fear the harvest would be wiped out, the cow would die, that illness would stop work or the lease would not be renewed. In short, that they would starve. Gentler instincts had to be rooted out and landlords, even neighbours, connived against in the struggle to survive. Religion could not provide sufficient comfort against so many woes and superstition was clung to as a further bulwark, to which might eventually be added alcohol.

Left: Millet's peasant woman carrying buckets.

Below: Paying the Harvesters, L. Lhermitte 1882.

Bread, the unceasing object of every peasant's life, was rye or mixed grains and sometimes buckwheat or chestnut flour. But of whatever composition, French peasants ate between two and three pounds a day, when they could get it — the largest consumption of bread in Europe. But this does not mean they ate more, rather that they ate very little else, the chief supplements being soup and when available salt pork.

For breakfast there was soup, usually onion or potato based, with a layer of bread in the bottom; though sometimes there was gruel. Soup was repeated at midday, possibly with beans or pumpkin in it, and in some areas there was cheese. In the evening, soup again — *'le souper'*.

Salt pork either in the soup or on slices of bread appeared as frequently as could be managed. Once a year most families killed a pig — a great occasion — and this was the only domestic animal regularly eaten.

Sundays and feast days usually brought improvements in the menu but butcher's meat was rare and Hélias recalls seeing chicken on the table no more than ten times in his youth, though the family was comparatively well off. Twice a week they had porridge, eaten from a common bowl. Each spoonful was dipped in milk to cool as everyone steadily made his way towards the centre where a big pat of butter lay, seeping slowly outwards.

But French country cooking as such is really a product of this century. After 1900, small grocery stores opened in villages, professional bakers appeared and sugar became available. Puddings with eggs and sugar appeared for the first time on Sunday tables and an increasing variety of dishes began to be cooked using those ingredients that form the base of France's regional cuisines: butter in the north and west, goose fat in the southwest and olive oil in the Mediterranean.

Another surprise is wine. An 1850 survey showed three-fifths of the country were strangers to it. Though wine was regularly consumed in towns, most peasants drank water or sometimes cider and sold what wine they made. Drinking it at home was largely the result of soldiers with new habits returning after World War I.

Although the community with its conforming checks and balances ruled rural life, families — or households — were the operative unit. Whatever the feelings within them, and they were often volatile, interdependence and gut attachment generally prevailed. But to belong to a household was above all to be a member of a workforce. At six or seven, children became shepherds or cowherds, taking the animals out at 5a.m. for three or four hours, then again in the evening. By fifteen, boys had assumed men's work and girls were already drilled in tasks that fell into the female sphere. But if there was not enough work at home boys were farmed out as young as ten years old and girls later on became domestic servants.

Hiring help was common practice on farms and in the mid-19th century accounted for half the labour force. Live-in help were part of the household, eating with the family, the girls sharing a bed with daughters and the men sleeping in the barn. Only at the end of the 19th century did big farmers in the north begin to seat their help at separate tables.

But despite the need for a strong workforce, disease, illness and deformity were commonplace. In 1860, for example, out of a thousand army recruits near Grenoble over half were rejected; goitre and humpbacks being prominent among their disabilities.

Personal hygiene was virtually unknown. Discarded clothes were piled in a corner of house or barn to await the great biannual wash — which was twice what people got: washing oneself was at best perfunctory and bathing virtually unheard of. 'I'm over 68 years old and never have I washed *there*,' declared a surprised Aveyronnaise woman in hospital.

Bed bugs and lice were indigenous and houses often damp and in poor repair, either because they belonged to others or because they were low on the list of priorities. 'It's not the cage that feeds the bird,' they said in the *bocage*.

Peasant dress with its striped trousers, beribboned skirts and elaborate, starched coifs such as are seen in prints and local museums were festive 19th century developments. Normally men wore baggy trousers with smocks made of hemp and wool, though after 1830 industrial cottons became increasingly available. By 1860 the blue blouse was universal but men usually had a linen shirt for Sundays.

Though women sometimes wore two or more skirts, neither sex reportedly wore proper underclothes before the 1880s. Nor did they have nightclothes: people slept in all or some part of their daily dress and work clothes were patched almost into second garments.

Wooden sabots are synonymous with peasant dress but a large number of people went barefoot, much to the surprise of Arthur Young, recording France's rural scene as the Revolution got underway. He also recorded the apathy that event inspired outside Paris. In Moulins no one was interested and it was impossible to get a newspaper. But then not only were most people illiterate but more than half the nation did not speak French, and this continued into the second half of the 19th century. Patois reigned and it was one of the great divides *and* insulators in rural communities.

But farm life essentially revolves around the seasons and the interminable tilling of the soil. In the mountains and on a number of tiny holdings this was done with a spade. Spades give superior aeration and mix the soil

Opposite page and above: scenes from peasant life sketched by Jean-Francois Millet in the 1860s.

better than a plough, but a man could not dig much ground in a year and the vast majority of farmers ploughed their land. Ploughing straight furrows took skill as well as energy; it also required a team of oxen or horses, which most peasants had to borrow. A two-horse team could turn up roughly an acre a day but once over lightly was never enough. A roller was required to break the clods and a harrow to rake the earth and leave a fine tilth. Fields were ploughed and harrowed four or five times in different directions, the seed sown by hand then covered by harrow and roller.

Fields were ploughed in spring and autumn but the busiest time of all of course was summer: no sooner was the hay mown, dried and loaded up than the corn was ready to be cut, followed by grape-picking in early autumn. Cereals were usually cut with a sickle; a man could reap 300 square metres in a day, and 500 square metres of herbage. But a scythe, when it was used, was roughly three times faster.

All available hands were needed at harvest time: men, women, children, families and neighbours worked together in teams and town holidays coincided so that the the townspeople too might help to gather that on which ultimately every life depended.

From November to February (All Saints day to Shrove Tuesday) the grain was threshed to remove the cereal from its stalk. 'I know of no work so exhausting,' wrote Emile Guillaumin*, describing the synchronized and unceasing rhythm with which a team of men flailed for most of the day, commencing again in the evenings, day after day. In parts of the south however the grain was trodden by oxen.

Winnowing was usually women's work, the chaff separated from the grain with sieves or by letting the wind blow it on to sheets.

Added to these largely male chores were ditch digging, pruning vines and fruit, fruit picking and wood cutting, cider and wine-making, lambing and cattle fairs. Each morning the oxen or horses had to be groomed and fed before being harnessed and this was repeated in the evening. On Saturdays the cowshed was cleaned out and new litter put down. In the evenings, if haymaking and flailing were done, tools and harness were mended and baskets woven. Yet as often as not men sought part-time work to make ends meet, taking on jobs at nearby farms, breaking stones for the roads or, as in Limousin, leaving home all winter to find work elsewhere.

To women fell the work of house, farmyard and vegetable garden. Wives got up between four and five a.m. to light the fire and prepare the morning soup. Fresh water had to be drawn from the well and, after the

A *winter* veillée.

* The Life of a Simple Man, the first published account of peasant life by a peasant, 1904.

dishes were washed, the cow was milked and slops cooked for the pig (though men sometimes did this). Often the woman took the cow to pasture and during the harvest she worked alongside the men, tying the sheaves and forking hay. Every year or two she gave birth, working right up to the event and as soon afterwards as possible. Many women died as a result of going back to work too soon, and when there was not a pregnancy there was usually a child to be nursed.

Women cooked, washed, brought in wood and looked after children. In the afternoon the cow(s) had to be milked again and the pigs and chickens fed. There was the vegetable garden and hemp patch to be tended as well as the baking and cheese and butter making.

In a number of regions women did not sit down with men at the table, but waited on them, eating afterwards from a bowl in the corner. Evenings were spent sewing and spinning and on Saturdays women went to market with their eggs and butter. Sundays were a day of rest but since most female tasks involved feeding others, few of their labours could be abandoned. Moreover, when men went to war, all tasks, male and female, fell on women and children.

And yet there was much gaiety. Celebration when it came was keenly felt, no doubt the more so for being richly deserved. Feast days, harvest dinners and above all marriages were scenes of great merrymaking. Marriage celebrations often lasted for days, during which dancing, bawdy jokes and above all eating and drinking were fully indulged. To fill one's stomach, that was the greatest joy, and yet they were so rarely able to do it. This final frustration of a food obsessed people is perhaps best illustrated by the boy who, weeping at a feast could eat no more. 'I'm full from top to bottom and yet I'm still hungry!' he cried. Everyone knew what he meant.

Another rural amusement was the winter *veillées*. People gathered in the evenings at one another's houses or in barns, as many as 20 or 30. Bringing handiwork to keep busy, they gossiped and listened to the tales and reminiscences that are one of the art forms of an oral culture. This enviable custom waned with the advent of village cafes which, to a degree, also separated the social lives of men and women.

Traditional peasant life finally disappeared only in the 1950s but its demise was anticipated nearly a century earlier. Increased communications and mass emigration to towns quickened change and removed people from their roots. Two world wars and the growing prosperity of a market economy accelerated changes. But the first notes of nostalgia for the old ways were sounded in the 1870s, and not by peasants, when the first folklore societies were founded. The aspic took some time to set.

Millet's The Sower *was produced in 1850.*

Woman Feeding her Child, J-F Millet 1861.

THE REGIONS

The regions included here are chiefly those of France's ancient provinces. Entities over a long period they developed a homogeneity not seen in the *départements* introduced during the Revolution. Many provinces were semi-independent duchies (Lorraine, Normandy, Provence and Brittany), others part of a foreign country (Flanders, Franche-Comté and Alsace), or even a different ethnic group (Basque). As a result the local architecture is sometimes sufficiently pronounced to have become synonymous with the province as a whole.

In others regions however – Ile de France and Burgundy for instance – no overall indigenous style exists, despite a common history. Instead there is a patchwork of many different styles, some no bigger than a locale or *pays*. This is because the soil, or presence of a river, marshland or mountain confined the area to a style not shared by those nearby. And in such cases the dominant or most unusual style has been singled out here.

Ironically perhaps France's history of warring fiefdoms and foreign acquisitions has resulted in the strongest vernacular styles being found along the country's outer edges: Brittany, Normandy, the Basque country, the Alps and Flanders and Alsace. With *architectural* boundaries however the reverse is true: like overlapping watercolours in a picture the purest shade is always at the centre, the edges a mélange of overlapping hues.

Since so many factors worked to establish regional styles it may be useful to review them. The subsoil and the fact that every farmstead falls into one of four basic categories (according to its layout) have already been discussed. So has the influence of chateaux and town architecture both on craftsmen and the general populace. The mode of farming was an important factor too, and clearly provincial traditions played a part. Imposed on this was the cultural divide between the north and south, roughly along the much-drawn line between St Malo and Geneva. Weak-sloped canal-tiled roofs was southern; steeply pitched roofs indigenous to the north. Different building materials also dominated both areas: the Roman tradition of stone work continued in the south, while cob or half-timbering – a Frankish tradition – generally ruled the north. After the 16th century however stone slowly began to replace clay wherever the subsoil made this possible.

Though it is true styles changed little over centuries, evolution nevertheless occurred and 'established traditions' are rarely as fixed as might appear. As we have seen, much of what is today 'traditional' only became so in the 19th century: central halls (where they exist), the use of lime instead of mud-based mortar, larger windows, terracotta floor tiles and slate and flat-tile roofs are some examples. No doubt the needs of modern life – bathrooms, sitting rooms, central heating and efficient kitchens – and the redundancy of outbuildings will continue to cause modifications; of which the most successful, in being copied, will become 'traditional'.

Fortified mill at Loubens in the Gironde.

ALPS

The mountain architecture of Savoy, Dauphiné and upper Provence is some of the most distinctive and robust in France. Often of vast dimensions, houses had to shelter under one huge roof a family, its livestock and enough provisions to see them through the long, bitterly cold winter months. Nowhere else in France has the interdependence of man and animals been more pronounced or until recently was it so intimate. An appreciation of these remarkable houses must therefore begin with the mode of life. Solidly pastoral it was centred on cows and ultimately on cheese.

Stone slab roof in the upper Maurienne valley (Savoy).

In the winter whole families, often several generations, were immured inside their houses. Looking after their animals, they were kept warm by them, in some places sharing the same room. Alternatively a communicating door allowed access without going outside.

But the alpine pastures were worth waiting for: the grass, though shorter, produced a superior nourishment and the exodus towards them began in May. Quite often it occurred in several stages or *remues*, the herd and shepherds stopping at way stations where small barns or chalets provided lodging and sometimes additional fodder.

Once in the high pastures however the herds combined, looked after by communal shepherds. Milking and cheese making fell to the women, as the men either stayed below or had to return there for haymaking – winter provisioning began almost at once.

But those who remained below generally moved to lighter, drier quarters upstairs, taking full advantage of the south-facing windows and broad balconies spanning the gable facades. Prime characteristics of mountain architecture, balconies were not for enjoying the view, serving rather as drying rooms and clothes-lines and as stores for wood and/or the dried dung used for winter fires.

The cut hay was stored in the house's vast loft space, loaded via earthen ramps usually built against the hillside. Vertically boarded gables with air spaces between the planks assured the ventilation necessary to prevent mildew or, in the case of grain, fermentation. In upper Provence, threshing floors were also in the loft. In parts of the Dauphiné however lofts were open at the sides to dry the crops.

Opposite: Savoy chalet made entirely of wood includes typical fretwork balcony. Chalets were often divided into two dwellings shared by kin.

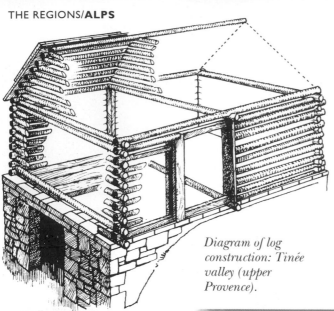

Diagram of log construction: Tinée valley (upper Provence).

Roofs are of great importance in mountain climates: they must keep out the damp and often support a heavy snowfall. Many alpine roofs are weak sloped and hold the snow for insulation; others are steep and throw it off. This discrepancy is not about different views on insulation. Since most alpine roofs were thatched until the 19th century a steep slope was needed to keep the thatch dry. But when wood, or in some places stone tiles –today's 'traditional' covering materials – replaced thatch, roof slopes could be broadened, and many were. Poles laid parallel with the eaves kept the melting snow from crashing down.

Two types of wood roofing, *tavaillons* and *ancelles* (see Roofing) were used. The shingle-like *tavaillon* is today seen mainly on the wind-exposed side of houses; *ancelles* (long overlapping planks) were much easier to repair and so retained their popularity. Larch was the favoured wood for roofing, lasting on average 20 to 30 years. Where gneiss and schist slabs *(lauzes)* were used, as in the upper Maurienne valley (Savoy), straw was often put under the tiles for insulation – a remnant of the earlier thatch.

Strictly, chalets are made of wood, preferably logs built up by overlapping at right angles. This type of building finds its purest form in northern Savoy (Chablais and Abondance valleys). The size of some of these houses is truly monumental, comprising in fact two houses. Divided along the ridgeline they were normally shared by kin. Two ramps in the rear give access to two haylofts and in the kitchens two huge funnel-shaped chimneys called *bournes* or sometimes *maisons* (see Franche-Comté for details), provided cooking facilities, ventilation and an escape hole when the house was buried in snow.

But wood, once in widespread use for building, was eventually proscribed in many areas. In the Maurienne and Tarantaise valleys for example an 18th century edict limited its use to balconies and roof timbers. A different style of house was the result. The rustic dwellings of these remote valleys are almost entirely of stone, including in the Maurienne, roofs – the huge *lauzes* capping low-built dwellings like a weighty platform.

Other areas such as the Beaufortin (Savoy) and Tinée valley (upper Provence) are a compromise: half wood, half stone. In the latter, log panels ventilate the loft and roofs are underpinned by a log-lining (see diagram).

The habit of keeping everything stored under one roof has an interesting exception. A separate log-built granary *(grenier)* one or two storeys high and sometimes covered with planks contained, in addition to grain, the family papers and valuables. Inspired by the fear of fire these walk-in chests, their doors set flush with the walls, also gave security against theft when families left their homes in summer.

Exotic Queyras (upper Provence) balconies were used for drying.

Opposite page:
Log granary built to store valuables and low, stone-built house with arched entrance and overhangng lauze roof, both at Bonneval-sur-Arc (Savoy).

Capacious farmstead in the middle Alps.

ALSACE

Alsatian houses are unique in France. Tall, half-timbered and rather medieval in feeling, their snub-nosed gables, gingerbread trim and strikingly colourful ornamentation have their true roots in Germany – and perhaps in fairytales, for storks' nests cap many a chimney pot and women wearing peasant dress can still be seen in the north.

Alsatian half-timbering or *colombage* has a pronounced rectangularity in which the upright and horizontal timbers are linked by slanting ones. The resulting patterns decorate and reinforce simultaneously, and many

Oxide dyes from the textile industry were traditionally used to colour houses. This example is in the famous Ecomusée (open air museum) at Ungersheim.

have a symbolic meaning, such as the popular 'man' symbols formed by a K or two Ks back to back.

Rudimentary half-timbering existed in Alsace in Roman times: the relative ease with which half-timbered houses could be reassembled suited a semi-nomadic life-style and ancient German law allowed houses to be sold separately from the ground they stood on. But the style's true refinement dates from the 17th century when a family of Swiss carpenters, the Schini, immigrated to Alsace. They brought with them a superior craftsmanship and such ornamental innovations as double balconies on gables and intricate half-timbered motifs under windows. In the following century the style attained its finest flowering: craftsmanship combined

Intricate timber motifs under windows date from the 17th century, and many are symbolic.

V pattern.

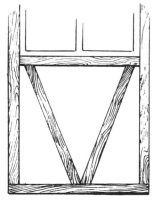

Lozenge and cross bar

Curule chair

with a growing economic prosperity to produce dwellings that were beautifully carved and painted inside and out. Two- and three-storeyed houses were constructed like a stack of boxes, each level separate from the one below. Vibrant colours, the feature that above all strikes the eye today, became popular at this time thanks to oxide dyes introduced by the textile industry. Houses were whitewashed or painted in cerulean blues, browns, yellows or terracotta reds, their oak timbers often darkened with walnut oil. Sometimes the framing timbers were outlined with coloured margins in the *torchis* or motifs were painted directly on the walls. Sometimes the *torchis* was very thickly applied, a technique known as *kratzputz,* or it was incised with coloured scraffito designs.

But colour and *colombage* are only a part of the special character of Alsation houses: their layout is equally noteworthy. Typically house and outbuildings are horse-shoed round a court (see page 31). The house faces the court with one gable overlooking the street, fronted by a narrow patch of garden. On this gable as often as not the family wealth and background are displayed, through decoration and inscriptions. Some gables sport opulent balconies, Schini style, with finely-turned balusters. Tiled awnings above the windows are another feature, especially in the Ried district.

Till the 19th century many houses had thatched roofs, which explains their steep slopes and flaring *coyaux.* However flat tiles began to be used in Alsace as early as the 1600s. Known as 'beaver tail' tiles because of their rounded ends, the tiles are gently grooved to better direct the flow of water.

Farms in the north and south differ somewhat in layout. In the more conservative south, the Sundgau, house and barn are joined at right angles instead of laid out round a court. But everywhere houses are large, built to shelter three generations plus domestics and farm hands; some farmsteads have a separate cottage for grandparents in the court.

The interior of Alsatian houses is as striking as their exterior. Unlike most of France the kitchen and sitting room are separate. The sitting room *(Stube)* faces the street, its corner windows overlooking both the street and interior court. Two benches at right angles were fixed underneath the windows and fronted by a table flanked by another bench or two. Called the *coin du Bon Dieu* (God's corner), a religious statue stood in a niche above. The family dined here, the men on the benches against the wall, the women and domestics on movable benches opposite.

Usually beautifully panelled and painted, the *Stube* gives on to a small alcove bedroom where master and mistress slept, or anyone who was ill. A smaller sitting room *(Kleinstube)* is sometimes found on the same floor. The other bedrooms are upstairs.

Each storey was constructed as a separate entity.

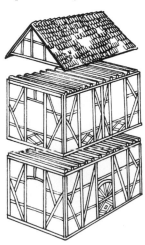

Nowhere are there open fires: stoves are used exclusively, an Alsatian practice going back to medieval times. A huge tiled or cast-iron stove (*Kachelofen*) in the *Stube* stands back to back with the kitchen cooker and was loaded from the kitchen (see diagram). Both stoves share the same chimney. Before the 19th century however many houses had no chimney: a vast hood covered both cooker and stove outlet and the smoke made its way out willy-nilly through the roof, smoking meat and sausages on the way.

The remarkable richness and variety of decoration in Alsation houses is today best seen in rebuilt farmhouses at the Ecomusée at Ungersheim, though almost every village has its fine examples, the large farmsteads at the centre, fringed by smaller fry, their fields and vineyards patchworked across the surrounding countryside.

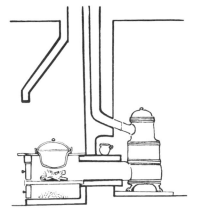

One chimney served both stove and cooker.

Tiled awnings over windows are a special feature of Alsace.

AUVERGNE

Located in the heart of the Massif Central, it is rock that gives this region much of its character. Huge granite blocks frame the windows and doors of houses with basalt walls blackened as by a fire. Even more spectacular are the old *lauze* roofs, heavy overlapping plates of schist or gneiss covering steep slopes like plated carapaces. Unfortunately there are not many left: most have given way to fishtail slates whose scale-like shimmer has a considerable charm of its own.

This is a region of remarkable contrasts and alongside houses of schist and basalt are to be found, especially in Livradois-Forez, those made of *pisé* or of pebbles. Equally *lauze* and slate roofs stand cheek by jowl with canal-tiled ones – the boundary between canal and flat tiles passes just north of Puy de Dôme. Proper Roman-style tiles can even be found around St Jean Lembron (see Roofing).

Building modes vary too but the most typical farmhouse is probably a type of *maison de maître* (master's house) found in the Carladez and Salersois areas of Cantal. Of imposing size, the steep, hipped roof is studded with a row of dormers topped by one or two further rows of tiny *houteaux.* Large chimneys rise at both ends of the house and, where gables are half-hipped, a graceful scooped effect enhances the overall silhouette.

Far left: high-houses like this one are plentiful in former winegrowing areas of the Auvergne.

Left: 'masters' houses' in the Cantal are distinguished by steep roofs studded with dormers and tiny houteaux.

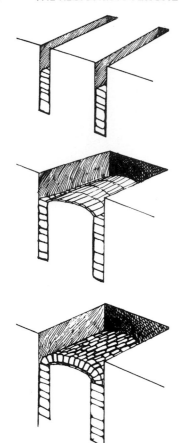

But the Auvergne was once a wine-growing region and there are also many high-houses with attractive wooden verandas and flat, canal-tiled roofs (stables having replaced the ground floor wine stores). An unusual and particularly charming feature is the small balcony or *plancadou* tucked under the roof above the main veranda, for storing chestnuts.

Other classic points are mammoth fireplaces, alcoves for kitchen sinks called *souillardes* (see Quercy) and, in the Limagne area, dovecotes. Noteworthy too are the stepped roof gables (Cantal) and vaulted underground *caves* built in the manner of ancient Egyptian vaults. Two parallel trenches were dug for the walls, as shown, and filled with stones and mortar; the vault was laid between them using the ground for support. A stair was then dug out and paved, and the soil between walls and vaulted roof removed.

Above: cellars were built by digging two trenches and using the ground to support vault during construction.

The Auvergnat barn or *grange-étable* is an efficient barn-cum-stable much imitated in neighbouring provinces. Two-storeyed and set against a hill, the animals entered at the lower level and their food at the top (via an earth ramp) where it could be forked down into the mangers. Roofs, originally thatched, are today covered in fishtail slates or *lauzes.* There is a pebble floor and, lined with mangers, the long stable walls are punctured by tiny windows

Depending on the area *granges-étables* are either attached to houses, in which case the doors are in the side wall , or freestanding with doorways in the gable. An interesting variation is the *burons* or *jasseries,* summer quarters for shepherds high in the mountains. Here the upper level is used for lodging, the lower reserved for cheese making.

Shepherd's quarters were smaller versions of Auvergnat barns.

Left: this finely-built granite farmhouse in the Margeride, dated 1844, is today a museum.

Below: classic longhouse with earthen ramp to barn.

THE BASQUE COUNTRY

The Basque word for house is *etche* and whether it fronts a village street or forms a dot on the green Pyrénéen foothills these huge whitewashed dwellings – often three storeys and sometimes longer than their great widths – are impressively solid.

Generally the facade is in the gable and the canal-tiled roof considerably overhangs the walls, especially in front. The main windows are also in the gable, the shutters and exposed timbers traditionally reddened with oxblood or painted deep green or brown.

An unusual feature of Basque houses is the *eskats* or *eskarats*. This large room entered by double barn doors was cartshed, tool room, threshing floor and an entrance hall off which other rooms opened. A stair against its wall leads to the upstairs lodging.

But the *etche* is not really a high-house. The oldest and poorest *etches* are often one storeyed and later houses kept a vestige of this plan in that the kitchen usually remained below. (According to Rodney Gallop, writing in the 1920s, it was not unusual to have two kitchens, one upstairs and one down, accommodating two possibly incompatible generations.) A parlour and bedrooms however developed upstairs in front of the hayloft, itself approached from behind by an earthen ramp, while an attic spanning the whole house contained the harvest, fronted by a balcony for drying.

Quite often the *eskarats* door was the only entrance to the house. Framed with dressed stone or a simple wooden lintel, one door panel was split horizontally to make a stable door.

Etche windows are small and sometimes wider than they are long; side windows are very small indeed, and the back of houses virtually blind. Floors, originally beaten earth, were later stone paved; though cement was favoured in the *eskarats,* or the beaten earth retained.

Of the three French Basque provinces, **LABOURD** *etches* are most typical. Built of rubble stone the upper facade is half-timbered and evidence suggests earlier houses were half-timbered throughout. It may therefore be that the remaining half-timbering is largely a superstitious tribute to the past. In any event its timber pattern is very simple: one row of widely-spaced upright posts.

Another feature of Labourdine *etches* is a recessed porch called the *lorio.* Set in one side of the gable or in front of the *eskarats* it made a sheltered workroom. Nowadays however the *lorio* is often enclosed as a garage or storage room.

Opposite: magnificent sandstone and granite doorway shows Moorish influence.

Arcane geometric motifs in champlevé *– the background cut away to make the design – decorate tombstones and houses.*

IOANNE S
DERRECALD E
ET MARGARITADE
CHURUTCHETMET
RE ET METRESSEDE
TCAHRT 1790

Above: Labourdine etche *at Ainhoa with half-timbered upper facade and recessed porch or* lorio.

Below: handsome stone-built farmhouse in the style of Basse Navarre.

In **BASSE NAVARRE** all half-timbering is dispensed with and the *etche* is entirely of stone. But the most remarkable feature of these houses is the *eskarats* doorway: some of them are monumental. A dressed sandstone surround rises in a sort of cone to join the stone frame of the window above. An inscription or decorative carving is in the middle. In some houses red and grey sandstone blocks alternate in an undoubtedly Moorish effect. These finely-built doorways, with dressed quoins and window surrounds set off by whitewashed walls, possess a refinement well above the rural norm.

Balconies are also common, especially in Cize and Bigorry.

SOULE is the highlands of the Basque country and for a time was joined to Béarn, whose architecture greatly influenced it. Gone is the *maison bloc*: there are outbuildings; but the *eskarats* remains and often it is still the only entrance. The stable though attached has a separate roof, giving the house a T or L shape depending on the point of attachment.

BEARN

From an architectural viewpoint it is the anomaly of Béarnaise roofs that draws most attention. Flat tiles and slates are a freakish blot in the traditionally canal-tiled south; but like most mountain houses those of Béarn were once thatched – which accounts for their steep roof pitch; and canal tiles would have slipped off.

Early Béarnaise houses were generally built of wood and clay. But in the 18th century a traveller noted that pebbles *(galets)* set in mortar was becoming popular, due no doubt to the increasing availability of lime mortar and decreasing availability of wood.

Many houses are fairly grand. Grouped in villages and disposed around closed courts, entry is through a gateway of impressive dimensions. On the plain of Nay outside Pau for instance the village streets are lined with huge two-storeyed farmsteads set in closed courtyards, sequestered worlds entirely sealed off from their neighbours. The houses face the court at right angles to the gateway; their pebble walls are rendered, their hipped roofs lined with dormers set above louvre-shuttered windows (rare in farmhouses). Over the door a decorative carving gives the construction date. Barns too are vast, with handsome arched entrances, sometimes two or three of them. Other outbuildings and a high wall complete the rectangle.

Elegant facade marks prosperous courtyard farmstead outside Pau.

131

In the maize rich prairie north of Oloron however houses tend to be L-shaped. The long arm of the L, parallel with the street, is pierced by an arched entrance running tunnel-like through the facade and into the courtyard. A wall completes the enclosure.

The west of Béarn is different – a region of transition with numerous smallholdings and *métairies*. Roofed in peach-coloured flat tiles, houses have their doors in the gable and the eaves are extended into wings, where the dwelling is found – the central 'aisle' with its large doors being the barn. *Génoises* are popular as cornices and the walls, often rubble limestone, are rendered.

Mountain villages along the Ossau and Aspe rivers maintain the older tradition of an upstairs lodging. The steep slate-covered roofs with their exaggerated *coyaux* look like vast sorcerers' hats festooned with dormers. A round bull's-eye window gives extra light to kitchens and quite often entry to the house is through the barn doors. (The arrangement mimics the Basque country next door.)

One of the most impressive villages is Beille, where medieval-looking houses, their stone mullioned windows adorned by carolling angels, date from the 16th century. Most houses open on to the street, their

Maison bloc *with lodging under one eave; the rest is carthouse and stable.*

Steeply pitched Beárnaise roofs, an anomaly in southern France, derive from thatched mountain houses.

entrance through great double doors into a carthouse with an earth floor. At one side a wooden staircase with an acorn finial leads to the lodging upstairs. The stable is behind the carthouse; the hayloft over it on a level with the dwelling. The fireplace consists of a huge hood suspended in a corner above the floor; and sometimes a bake oven is attached at first floor level by corbelling.

Though the 18th century produced the Béarn house as we know it, it was 19th century prosperity – spas, maize, wine and horses – that resulted in its enlargement and the use of flat tiles and slates instead of thatch. The arrival by rail of coal for the kilns and better tools (from England), helped make such improvements efficient and relatively cheap.

BERRY

The plain of Champagne Berrichon with its large enclosed *métairies* dominated by vast barns and fringed by smallholdings – or *locatures* as they are called – is Berry's heartland. This is a region of limestone, large brick chimneys, dormers with ladders, and flat tiles that have been used here since the Middle Ages.

Houses are normally one-storeyed and squarish in shape with broad overhanging roofs. An oven and sometimes a pigsty is attached to the gable. Typically houses are one-roomed, the spacious *salle* five or six metres wide and seven metres long is spanned with oak beams cut as a rule when trees were thirty years old.

There are also two-roomed *métairies* but these date from the mid-19th century.

Floors in the north are paved with stone tiles *(dalles)* and in the south terracotta tiles. A huge fireplace dominates the room, hooding a stone hearth flush with the floor (though later fireplaces sometimes have raised hearths).

Opposite page: brick-trimmed farmhouse with classic dormer and attached barn.

Left: overhanging flat-tiled roof and ladder to dormer are fully in character; the half-timbered wall visible under the eaves denotes the Pays Fort and Solonge.

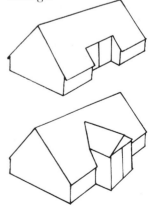

Older barns have recessed entrances in the Pays Fort but porches in Champagne Berrichon.

Open-court manorial farmstead with dovecote, mellowed by age and disrepair.

Berrichon barns (see page 91) are of particular interest. The oldest are aisled hall constructions with walls some five feet high, the steeply pitched roofs either thatched or covered in flat tiles. Many date from the late 15th to the 17th centuries and the oldest have their entrances in the gable. A number of barns have a porch for unloading vehicles but in the Pays Fort the reverse is true and entrances are recessed, as shown.

The Pays Fort and Solonge areas which fringe the plain are dotted with quaint half-timbered houses usually infilled with brick, their steep roofs covered in rosy flat tiles that together with simply-constructed dormers are such an appealing feature of this ancient province.

BRITTANY

Breton houses are fascinating: not only is their regional character pronounced but, thanks to a strongly rooted past, extant houses recapitulate the entire history of French domestic habitation. There exist today as sheds and pigstys buildings identical to dwellings that once housed most of Europe's population. Known as *lokenn* or *loges,* these primitive shelters look like thatched roofs sitting on the ground and a few were still inhabited in the 1940s (a hole in the roof emitting smoke from

Renaissance-style window displays the fine carving in granite found on manors and religious monuments (calvaries) throughout lower Brittany.

the central hearth). Later examples had low stone walls to improve headroom, as walls were invented to do; but their corners were rounded – true corners being harder to build.

By the 16th century however most Breton walls had reached a normal height and the fireplace had begun its move to the gable, where a clay chimney drew out smoke. But houses still had only one room: the family living at one end, their cow tethered at the other– in other words, a primitive version of the classic longhouse (see Basic Types).

BRETON LONGHOUSES were roughly 30 feet long and 15 feet wide. Early ones had a central door through which both man and beast entered en route to their respective ends. The dwelling end had a small window and, if possible, occupied the upper slope; otherwise a drain covered by stones ran beneath the earth floor. Eventually another door was set in the back wall opposite the first, creating a sort of walkway demarcated by linen chests on one side and feed troughs on the other. A ceiling of hazel or chestnut sticks rolled in *torchis,* then covered with beaten earth, created a loft.

Opposite page: thatched house with stair to upper lodging in the preserved village of Poul-Fetan (Morbihan). Note that each step is a single stone.

Below: granite farmhouse and attached barn are crowned by handsome dormer pediments.

Matched doors to stable and lodging are typical of Ille-et-Vilaine.

Extraordinary 19th century 'menhir' stone cottages suggest the survival of primitive religious beliefs.

In the 18th century a wooden waist-high partition was erected on the dwelling side of the walkway, further demarcating the living area. In the next century this became a full partition and a second chimney sprouted in the opposite gable. Influenced no doubt by the fashion for symmetry, another motive was the peasants' belief that cows must see the fire to give good milk.

But by the 19th century most houses had a separate stable door and all interior connection between stable and dwelling had vanished. Both types remain plentiful however, though the former is usually given over entirely to livestock now.

MANORS were the earliest two-room plan Breton dwellings and from the 16th century the rooms were divided by a corridor. One room was used by the seigneur and family, the other by their domestics. A turret staircase led to another pair of rooms upstairs, often with fireplaces; but these were workrooms not bedchambers when they were built.

Manor house doorways are elegantly appointed with chamfered, finely-carved arches or huge megalithic surrounds (many a menhir has been incorporated into the walls of houses). A stable, barn, sheepfold, cider mill and sometimes a chapel complete the compound in front of the house.

Small manors of this sort are by no means rare: nearly two thousand were built in Côtes du Nord – now Côtes d'Amor – alone. Later most became peasant farms and the new owners, keeping to peasant tradition, occupied only one room and used the rest for storage.

TWO-ROOM FARMHOUSES with a central corridor first appeared in coastal areas in the 18th century. Spreading slowly inland they became widespread after World War I. Many of these were modified longhouses and the second room, a parlour, was rarely used; though a bed or spinning wheel might sometimes find its way there.

PENTY This one-roomed cottage built to house agricultural workers or, on larger farms, an overseer (and sometimes fishermen) had a loft but no provision for animals. The occupants had none. The *penty's* cube-like proportions are visually very pleasing and on the south coast white-painted walls and bright blue shutters give them a special gaiety. Today the word *'penty'* is becoming synonymous with cottages generally.

HIGH-HOUSES with lodging on the first floor were built in Brittany in the 17th century and quite often they comprised *two* dwellings. The lord, who visited his property to hunt or to collect the rents, was lodged upstairs and the peasant family and their livestock occupied the ground floor as a longhouse. An exception was the Léon area where ground floors became workrooms for the linen industry.

OUTSHOTS An outshot is a protruding niche or alcove built to accommodate the family bed and/or board – and so make more room for spinning. Found around Léon, outshots for a table or box bed and table are in the facade, those exclusively for beds are at the back and windowless.

ROW HOUSES comprising from two to a dozen dwellings – with or without connecting doors – lodged several families. A connection between this type of building and nearby communal fields has been pointed out by the architectural historian Gwyn Meirion-Jones.

'MENHIR' HOUSES These dwellings, located around Pont Aven and Concarneau (southern Finistère) are extremely interesting. Built in the

Tufted thatch, arched doorway and megalithic granite framing stones – a classic example of local architecture. Poul-Fetan (Morbihan).

19th century, their walls are a row of menhir-like granite slabs some two and a half metres tall (half a metre is buried to keep them upright). White clay mortar between the slabs gives the houses a curious striped appearance. The roof is thatched and hipped at one end and the chimney gable is of rubble stone.

MUD HOUSES A word must also be said about the clay-built houses of the Rennes basin. Constructed in *bauge* (see Materials), the clay lumps were lifted on to the walls with pitchforks. Alternatively adobe was used. Today many *bauge* and adobe houses no longer have their exterior walls rendered and the warm colour of the exposed clay can be very appealing.

In addition to *types* of houses a number of specific features characterise Breton architecture. Grey and rose granite, also schist and sandstone, were

the main building materials and doors and windows are often framed with cyclopean granite slabs. Renaissance arches, introduced in the 16th century, are frequent too and houses in the northeast (Ille-et-Vilaine) have a pair of arched doors giving entry to stable and house respectively. Some of these houses have second storeys.

Roofs are generally two-sloped and, though thatch is seen in the Grande Brière, slate is ubiquitous, but even these roofs have retained their gable parapets built originally to protect thatch.

Breton windows are small and few. Where a dormer exists it is usually over the front door. Glazing was rare before the mid-19th century and wooden bars or oiled linen was used or, in richer houses, iron basket grills.

Beaten earth floors, once common throughout Brittany, have mostly been concreted over.

Fisherman's penty *locked between boulders at Plougrescant (Côtes d'Amor). The region is famous for its rose-pink granite.*

143

BURGUNDY

The riches of its religious and seigneurial past easily eclipse vernacular buildings in Burgundy. The more so since no single, dominant regional style exists. The only farmhouse found everywhere is a four-square hipped roof dwelling with a symmetrical facade, louvred shutters and sometimes a dovecote attached. Weather vanes and *épis* add to its ostentation. Most of these houses were built in the late 19th century by rich farmers – *paysans aisés.* They were copied from the bourgeoisie who had in turn copied them in the 18th century from the *petite noblesse.* The style proliferated, especially in southwest Burgundy, when railways opened the Paris markets to Charollais beef.

The Auxois, also a wealthy stockbreeding area, has many big houses too. Huge stone-paved *salles* and dark brown flat-tiled roofs are typical. Flat tiles were introduced in Burgundy by monks in the 11th century, becoming widely known as Burgundian tiles; but today, even in the Auxois, they are disappearing in the wake of modern mechanical tiles.

The wine-growing regions of Côte d'Or and the Mâconnais favour high-houses, with marked stylistic differences in each area. In the Mâconnais for instance stairs are perpendicular to the facade in the north and parallel to it in the south, protected by an awning set on sculpted wooden posts. Sometimes a second gallery spreads above the first. Côte d'Or stairs on the other hand run parallel with the facade and have no awning.

Cattle-breeding financed the large bourgeois-style houses of the Charollais.

Moreover, Mâconnais houses are enclosed in courts (general farming being carried on in addition to viticulture) while Côte d'Or houses are set at right angles to the street, accessible by a narrow drive. The lodging often contains an alcove wash room or *souillarde* and the *cuvier,* where wine is made, is contiguous with the house.

Finally, Côte d'Or *caves* are vaulted and Mâconnais *caves* are not.

Though fine limestone is the chief building material in Burgundy, the east and northwest are an exception. In the latter, around Sens, Othe and the Puisaye, chalk and flint were used rendered over and the windows and doors framed with bricks. In Sens, the brick patterns connect the windows and doors. Brick was also used as infill for the delightful veranda-fronted houses of Bresse Louhannaise (see Lyonnais), and for houses in the Saône valley less than a century old.

Brick trim is popular in the stone-free north, especially around Sens.

High-houses dominate Burgundy's winegrowing regions.

CHAMPAGNE

Champagne is geologically – therefore architecturally – split into two regions: 'dry' and 'wet'. These have nothing to do with drink. 'Dry' Champagne refers to the chalk plain from which the region takes its name (*champagne* originally meant a limestone plain) and before chemical fertilizers this one was wretchedly poor, covered with porous chalk and given over to rye and sheep.

'Wet' Champagne, lying along the eastern boundary, was more prosperous. Its heavily wooded clay soil, rivers and many pools attracted monasteries early in the Middle Ages – and with them a developed tradition of stockbreeding.

But in both regions farmers had to build with what there was: chalk and adobe on the plain; clay and wood, *i.e.* half-timbering, in 'wet' Champagne.

Chalk was quarried by the peasants in winter and left underground for use in the spring; but its quality was very uneven. Denser grades could be cut into handsome lard-like blocks, excellent for building, while lesser qualities were sometimes suitable for rubble wall construction. Otherwise adobe proved a better bet. Popular in the Marne valley east of Épernay the clay was moulded into hefty 'bricks' weighing about two kilos each. A heavy lime content made them unusually strong.

Chalk was used extensively in building houses and barns in western Champagne.

*Tall half-timbered houses
with flat canal-tiled roofs
epitomize the east. Note
stone drain from sink,
beside door in the
photograph.*

But whether adobe or chalk was used, burnt bricks invariably framed windows and doors – a style readily familiar across the chalky northern plains.

But it is half-timbering, not chalk with brick trim, that has given Champagne architecture notoriety. Plainer and less refined than in Normandy or Alsace the rusticity of Champagne *colombage* has a special charm. The timber posts are always simply disposed, their upright lines broken by occasional oblique timbers and the horizontal beams at floor and ceiling levels. Though *torchis* is the normal filling adobe and chalk were also used, and a number of houses have solid chalk gables. Brick was the favourite material for chimneys.

Two different roof styles divide half-timbered houses in the north and south, producing very different effects. In the north, paradoxically, canal tiles are used, and the shallow roof capping a rather tall and narrow half-timbered rectangle makes a silhouette that is uniquely Champagnoise. (Some older roofs have kept their Roman-style tiles.)

In the south however roofs are steeply pitched and clad in dark flat tiles punctuated with handsome dormers – the overall appearance is faintly similar to Normandy farmhouses.

Most houses were built in villages and closed courtyards are the dominant plan. In 'dry' or chalk Champagne entry is through a covered gateway but in the east many half-timbered houses have a *porche à porte rue*: double doors in the facade open to make a passage through the house into the courtyard behind where, with the other outbuildings, there is a large barn.

Champagne barns are very impressive. The oldest and most interesting are between the Aube and Seine where, in addition to low walls and a vast roof, a large porch exists for threshing and sheltering waggons.

FLANDERS & PICARDY

The soil of Flanders and Picardy is predominantly clay and chalk and for centuries half-timbering was the traditional method of building. In the 18th century however brickmaking began to spread in Flanders: improved firing methods and increasing wealth making it available to farmers. Soon brick had superseded *colombage.* But this did not occur in Picardy. Today therefore more than any other factor different materials separate the two regions architecturally.

In both provinces houses are long and low, prefiguring modern bungalows. Many houses are set in small courtyards, a distinctive double chimney rising in the centre of the high-pitched roofs. Outbuildings are joined or separate and a few large farms have – as does neighbouring Champagne – horse mills housed in special octagonal buildings.

Brick sawtooth motif, here on chalk gable.

Bakehouse turned chickenhouse shows composite walling of brick and chalk roofed in pantiles.

But the feature that above all characterizes this area is its roofing material: pantiles. Thought to have been invented in Ghent, pantiles began to replace thatch in Flanders and Picardy in the 18th century. Because pantiles overlap laterally they are watertight, adding to their appeal on a plain dominated by ever-changing skies. A warm apricot colour or when varnished deep aubergine, pantiles add considerably to the region's extraordinary colourfulness.

So do bricks: rose, yellow or dark brown (depending on the part of Flanders), brick was most often laid in a pattern called *Kruisverband,* consisting of a row of headers (short ends) alternating with a row of stringers (long sides) – in other words English not Flemish bond (see Brick). Some brick houses are whitewashed, as are all the half- timbered houses of Picardy; and everywhere shutters are gaily painted in contrast with the tarred foundations that protect houses from damp.

Picardy *colombage* differs significantly from neighbouring Normandy and Champagne in that houses are completely rendered and, instead of adding decoration to the facade, the timber frame is totally hidden from view. Again colour is relied on for any decorative effect.

Though most farmhouses are 18th and 19th century, several older traditions have been preserved. Gables receive special attention. Stepped gables can still be found, recalling the earlier thatch, and some brick gables are decorated with 'runes', geometric symbols whose origins go back at least a thousand years. Another distinctive feature is alternating bands of stone and brick *(rouge barre)* or chalk and stone *(en larde).* But the most pervasive gable treatment is 'saw-teeth' in which bricks are set at right angles to the gable eave, as shown, to create a smooth edge. The practice may have been a means of making gables watertight.

Another special feature of Flanders houses is the 'high chamber'. This room, often a parlour, is located above a semi-basement with an unusual ceiling. The spaces in between the supporting beams are cradle-vaulted in brick. This technique is also found in stables and, occasionally, farmhouse ceilings (the brick concealed under a coat of plaster). But the reason for such elaborate construction is unclear.

A word must also be said about the huge farmsteads called *censes* found in Artois and around Lille. Courtyard farmsteads, their impressive gateways are often topped by dovecotes or a dovecote stands sentinel in the court. Some farmsteads are moated by rectangular trenches, today a useful means of watering cattle.

Similar farmsteads in Flanders are called *hofsteds,* while in the Boulonnais hills are a number of manor-like farmhouses that, having once divided life between wars and agriculture, often have a fortified tower and machicolations.

Motifs used to decorate brick gables.

Picardy farmsteads are by tradition rendered and finished with colourful trim; the foundations are tarred.

FRANCHE-COMTE

In the Jura mountains along the eastern border of Franche-Comté is a house very closely related to alpine dwellings. Called a *maison à tué* it is vast, square and gable fronted. The ground floor is stone-built (sometimes the first floor too) and the gable above boarded with lengths of overlapping planks called *lambrissures*. Three to five lengths in height, spaces between the planks give the huge hayloft its ventilation. Entry to the loft is by an earthen ramp at the rear and the loft also contains a threshing floor. The broad low roof is by tradition covered with shingles – *ancelles* or *tavaillons* (see Roofing) and, as in the Alps, many houses are divided along the roof ridge to make two dwellings.

But it is the fireplace that has made these houses famous. Called a *tué,* it is a combination room, fireplace and chimney. Consisting of a giant square funnel several metres square at the base and built of horizontal planks nailed to four upright posts, the funnel ascends to the roof where the short stack is capped by two flaps opened and closed by cords from

Earthen ramp gives access from hilltop to farmhouse loft. The plank-cladding allowed crops to be aired via spaces between the boards.

below. The fire was built on the floor – for the *tué* is in fact a remnant of the primitive hut with a central hearth once common throughout Europe. Similar chimneys in Bresse and southern Savoy are called *huteaux* and *maisons* respectively – words that bespeak their history.

The *tué* also made an efficient smokehouse: hams and sausages were hung from poles inside the funnel and as the chimney drew out smoke it smoked the meat; it also let light into the windowless room below. In addition when the house was buried in snow the funnel provided an emergency exit. Finally the *tué* functioned as a foyer, doors to the *poêle* (see below), stable, *cave* and bread oven opening off it – and *foyer* in French *means* 'fireplace'.

Unlike most French farmhouses, *maisons à tué* have a large number of rooms – sometimes as many as nine. Directly behind the *tué* is the *poêle,* the room reserved for intimate family occasions and where husband and wife slept in a curtained bed. Another bedroom is sometimes found on either side of the *poêle.* In addition many farmsteads had a workroom or *atelier* where during the winter months the immured herdsmen transformed themselves into craftsmen. The longcase clocks that during the 19th century became standard furnishings in French houses were mostly made by 'cottage' artisans in Franche-Comté.

The oldest *maisons à tué* are in the canton of Montbenoit (Doubs), around Saugat; but excellent specimens can be seen too in the *Musée de plein air des maisons comtoises* at Nancray, where old farmhouses from throughout the province have been painstakingly reassembled.

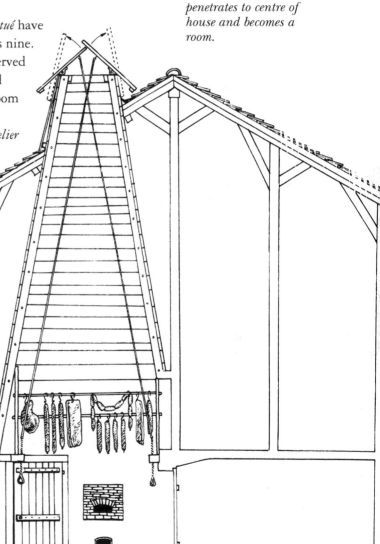

Tué *chimney funnel penetrates to centre of house and becomes a room.*

GUYENNE & GASCONY

Limestone is the main building material in Guyenne* and its colour and quality are diverse: soft easy-to-cut honey-coloured stone, hard white rubble stone and grey, friable tufa – depending on the spot. But half-timbering is also seen and, in the Garonne valley, composite walling and brick.

Canal-tiled, Guyenne roofs generally have incurving (see page 51) and the gables are often hipped. But because the hip has a steeper pitch it is covered with flat tiles. A *génoise* borders the eaves.

But the really fascinating thing about these farmsteads is the various ways in which house, stable and barn are accommodated under one roof. For here the *maison bloc* probably finds its greatest elaboration.

Traditional longhouse, half house, half barn-cum-stable, with a door for each.

*For our purposes limited to the departments of Lot et Garonne and the Gironde. Perigord, Quercy, Rouergue and the Landes have separate entries.

Verandas are ubiquitous in Guyenne. Attached to walls or gables, the supporting posts were mounted on stone footings or a low wall.

Three main forms are found (see also Basic Types). One is the traditional longhouse which, though similiar to *bocage* longhouses further north, is twice their width. Dwelling and barn are separated by a wall, the latter further partitioned into carthouse and stable. Three doors in the facade accommodate man, vehicles and livestock – the barn doors arched attractively. Houses of this type are generally one-and-a-half storeys, the loft aired by small windows – round, square, oval or lozenge shaped – and known locally as *fenestrous.* A pigsty and prune oven may also be attached to the house.

The second type of *maison bloc* is gable-fronted and divided into three parts *parallel* with the long walls. The carthouse is in the centre, the dwelling under one eave and the stable under the other. A *chai* is usually at the back.

The third form puts the dwelling in front and the stable and barn at the rear, the facade being either a gable or long wall.

In all three forms the entire loft functioned as part of the barn and was used to store hay, tobacco and other crops.

The oldest gable-fronted farmsteads have two-sloped roofs spread as broadly as possible over low walls, resembling squat versions of alpine chalets. But in later versions gables are often snub-nosed and some have a recessed loggia – as in the Landes next door – making a useful and inviting veranda. Alternatively the long walls may be extended forward to make a gable veranda the width of the house.

A number of wall-facaded houses also have verandas, supported by posts set on stones or a low wall. The region's many verandas and loggias are attributed by some historians to Italian influence when, after the Italian wars, local lords brought Italian craftsmen back home with them.

Dovecotes are plentiful and varied. Usually square and occasionally hexagonal, a few rest gracefully on pillars or even straddle gables above the loggia.

Right: gable-fronted farmhouse near Tonneins: the steeple-like dovecote helps to create a loggia.

Below: older maisons blocs *were often low-lying, their roofs stretching across the widest possible space like the wings of a brooding hen.*

But not every house is a *maison bloc* and in the east and Garonne valley a separate barn is customary. Open-fronted with large timbers in the upper gable, the roof ridge is supported by a central post, reminiscent of a vast nomadic tent. Intriguing to see, these structures were useful for drying tobacco; also plums, as a prune oven was usually set in the gable underneath one eave.

Peaked facades like this are a regular feature of the Gers.

The Bordeaux region, rich in wine chateaux and *chartreuses* (as one-storeyed gentlemen's residences are called), contains a farmhouse of unusually refined character. Constructed of creamy limestone cut into dressed blocks the style resembles dwellings along the Loire. An elegantly moulded stone cornice and a decorative stone band at ceiling height express a prosperity beyond the normal reach of peasants. *Fenestrous* in the loft are round or square and in pleasing proportions to the windows below. The rear of houses was often extended to include the *chai,* the canal-tiled roof descending to within a few feet of the ground.

Even tiny artisans' cottages and huts in vineyards are constructed in this manner.

GASCONY was a province of petty *seigneuries* and its heartland, the Gers, is still one of the most rural areas in France. It contains many ancient manors and chateaux and, though no vernacular style is dominant, the most distinctive is probably a square, one-storeyed dwelling with a four-sloped canal-tiled roof. Constructed of rendered limestone, a triangular pediment over the door contains the entrance to the loft.

There are also many two-storeyed houses in the Gers, and many dovecotes.

Honey-coloured Gironde farmhouse constructed of ashlar limestone.

ILE DE FRANCE

The vernacular styles in Ile de France are a testament to the extraordinary diversity of the sub-soil: millstone in Brie, quality limestone in the Soissonnais, clay and rubble limestone on the Beauce and plaster of Paris in the Paris basin are examples. And though much of the area round Paris has been rebuilt with modern materials, older traditions survive in the outer circle – most notably in the large courtyard farmsteads of the plain. Grouped in villages or sited on the expanse of open ground they are enclosed by extensive outbuildings of enormous length. Some of the largest are in Soissonnais, Brie and the Vexin, their size equal to that of small villages. In fact they once enjoyed a similar composition, housing workmen and providing bakery, cartwright, laundry and the other appurtenances of a self-contained community.

Right: grand entrance gate to wealthy Soissonnais courtyard farmstead. Note tethered goat in foreground.

Renaissance-style dormer pediment.

A number of farmsteads, especially in Brie, are fortified. Originally appendages of local abbeys and *seigneuries,* they are enclosed by high walls with entrance through the doors of a grand gate. A chapel and dovecote are sometimes present too. Built to accommodate mixed farming, farmsteads like these were adapted to cereal culture in the 18th century and, quite frequently, sugar beet in the 19th – becoming what the French call *fermes usines* (factory-farms). Their acreage was for 19th century France immense – 100 to 400 hectares.

Surprisingly, the farmhouses are not themselves particularly large; it is the long line of outbuildings that conveys such an impressive monumentality. An exception is the Soissonnais where quite grand houses do exist, two storeyed and built of dressed limestone, with louvred shutters, and a dovecote rising in the centre of the court.

Roofs are generally two-sloped and covered in flat tiles (or slates), the ridgeline tiles secured with plaster of Paris. The striped effect of plaster joints along the roof ridge is a well-known feature of the region. Another is the use of dormers. Many of these have pulleys attached to lift up crops; some are faced with an elegant *fronton* and a number display curved Renaissance-style pediments, as shown. Even today ladders can be seen propped against dormer doors – still the only access to the loft.

Chimneys too are varied. Brick chimneys are much in evidence but in the Soissonnais – where stepped gables were the fashion – dressed stone chimneys were carefully tailored to complete the stairstep shape. But chimneys were also set in the middle of houses.

Caves, often vaulted, were dug underneath the house or, in some cases, in the garden.

A huge courtyard farmstead spread village-like across the Brie plain.

Stair-step chalk gable takes chimney stack in its stride.

THE LANDES

Before the mid-19th century the Landes was largely an agro-pastoral community. The word *landes* means 'heather' and in the summer myriad flocks of sheep and goats grazed the open moors watched by shepherds in rough fleeces, standing on stilts so as to see their animals at a distance. Rye, millet and maize were grown on the *métairies,* a little hemp and flax and in some areas vines.

Then in 1857 everything changed. A huge pine forest encompassing over two million acres was planted by decree: its purpose, to secure the shifting sand dunes of the Landes floor and to introduce timber-farming which the new railway would make profitable.

Bereft of grazing lands however the sheep and goats rapidly disappeared, followed by the local crops; since without animals they could not be fertilized. Many peasants turned to timber-related work, principally *gemmage,* tapping trees for resin to make turpentine. But fluctuating prices made the industry unreliable and soon the timber lords discovered that what they had in fact created was a gigantic matchbox. Repeated forest

Classic Landaise farmhouse with gable facade, a showpiece at the Ecomusée (open air museum) in Marqueze.

fires and large-scale unemployment resulted in mass emigration so that today the population of the Landes is half of what it was in 1900.

Yet the traditional Landaise farmstead is one of the most enchanting habitats in France. Located near villages in the forest, it comprises a small group of buildings shaded by a canopy of splendid oaks. This beautiful oasis is called an *airial* – the word is Gascon – and its centrepiece is a ghostly half-timbered house, the gable facade deeply recessed to create a cool and welcoming veranda cordoned by a low wall or picket fence.

The veranda *(estantad* or *balet)* faces east, making it a fine spot to sit and do one's work morning and afternoon, the railings keeping animals and children in or out as desired. A stairway against one wall (or sometimes indoors) gives on to a balcony above. Here crops and clothes could be dried shielded from the rain and wind. In the apex of the gable naturally curved oak timbers are used to great effect, and it is not unusual to see the construction date writ large on one of them.

Most of the houses now extant are 19th century, though some are a century older. Their phantom-like appearance is due to limewash painted on walls and timbers alike as a protection against insects and fungus.

Secondary timbers are simply positioned and the windows small and squarish: few had glass, merely wood bars or removable panels. The broad canal-tiled roof is often three-sloped and known as *'queue de palombe'* or pigeon's tail – a reference derived from the local passion for shooting these birds when the season begins each year in mid-October.

The *salle* or livingroom is a big square room, its hearth hooded by a vast chimneypiece. This room is both kitchen and a kind of hall, since the

Shepherds traditionally watched their flocks from stilts.

Above left: this half-timber patterning resembles an abstract painting.

Landaise veranda makes an extra room.

Not all Landaise farmhouses are gable-fronted with recessed verandas. Note the Roman roof tiles.

other rooms – as many as six of them – open off it. Both the hearth and *estantad* floor are a continuation of the tiled floor of the *salle,* though initially these would have been of beaten earth.

A very original feature of the *salle* is a little window at right angles to the fireplace. The window gives on to the *ristoun,* a small stable used in winter to fatten one or two cows or bullocks. Their heads were slotted through the window, as in a milking stall, and the animals hand-fed by a family member sitting comfortably beside the fire.

Several wooden outbuildings are scattered about in no particular fashion; the most remarkable of which is the chicken house, a square construction mounted on stilts (see Outbuildings). But the sheepfold was an important building too. Weatherboarded inside and out, often with a thatched roof, the west side had a covering of brush to protect and insulate the building. There was also a summer *bergerie.* This isolated building had a low-reaching three-sided roof; a room with a brick chimney provided lodging for the shepherd.

Though not all farmhouses had gable facades, a few had them on both ends – with two kitchens set back to back. These were either shared *métairies* or lodgings for both the landlord and his tenant.

Farmhouse sink lit by wood-barred window.

The best place to see a Landaise *airial* complete with traditional furnishings and outbuildings is the Ecomusée at Marqueze. An old-fashioned train leaves Sabres regularly on the ten minute journey to the forest clearing.

LANGUEDOC, ROUERGUE, CEVENNES

Throughout Rouergue and the Cévennes mountains and along the vine rich plain of Languedoc high-houses predominate, the ground floors used as storage, sheepfold or *chai* according to need. The houses are built of schist and granite in the mountains and limestone on the plain and great dry *causses* of the north. Schist was also used as roofing in the mountains and *causses;* while on the plain and in the Cévennes valleys, canal tiles proclaim the ancient traditions of the south.

But the most striking architectural feature of this somewhat diverse region is the use of arches and vaults. Stone 'bridges' curved like rainbows connect thresholds to hillside slopes and cradle arches form galleried arcades supporting first floor terraces. Some vaults rise from ground to roof

Large derelict mas *on the Languedoc plain with distinctive cradle-vault foundations.*

*Granite mountain
house in the Lozère
(Cévennes) boasts an
impressive staircase to
upper storey.*

*Below: the use of
arches is well-
illustrated, and
includes the peaked
windows, in this
farmstead on the
Grand Causse
plateau.*

ridge, terminating in a gothic point or top another arch to make a second storey. Cradle vaults, groined vaults and corbelling are all used and walls a metre thick help to take the stress. But the laborious construction involved is hardly justified by a need for structural support and one cannot help wondering if entrenched Roman custom hasn't played a part.

Rainbow arch to loft.

In the uplands few houses are rendered; thick walls and small windows guard against the cold. In the Rouergue, windows are capped by points in the roof line that create an attractive saw-tooth decoration along the eaves. A very remarkable roof style exists around Mende. Called *à la Philibert* after its 16th century inventor, it is a masterpiece of carpentry. Built on a system of wooden arches that seem almost to mimic the stone cradle vaulting of the region, the effect is of an inverted ship's hull, and a vast and unencumbered storage space results.

In the low-lying Languedoc plain carpeted with vineyards the atmosphere is very different. Large *mas,* as farmsteads are called, rise fortress-like among the vines and several along the coast are fortified, protecting the original occupants from pirates.

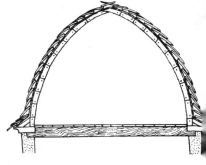

Undulating vaulted roofline in the Rouergue.

Rendered and sometimes whitewashed, *mas* are normally enclosed in courts, often vast enclaves that bring to mind the magnificent Roman villas they have replaced. Built to accommodate mixed farming, most of these huge establishments have been carefully adapted to the needs of viticulture, and large *chais* lit by crescent shaped *jours* take prominent place among the outbuildings.

But not all farmhouses on the plain are *mas.* Smaller dwellings abound, normally fronted by two doors: an arched one giving entry to the *chai,* the other to an inside stair ascending to the living area.

Philibert roof.

The switch from polyculture to viticulture in lower Languedoc was paralleled by similar changes earlier in the Cévennes. Too acidic for growing cereals, chestnuts were planted in the Middle Ages in lieu of rye. Known as 'bread trees', the fruit when picked had to be quickly dried and special ovens were built in the form of two-storeyed bakehouses. (see Outbuildings). In the 18th century however the chestnut trees were devastated by a blight and a new crop had to be found. This time it was a money crop: silk. Mulberry trees were planted on hand-built terraces up the hillsides and special apartments called *magnaneries* were set up in attics, or sometimes in a special building. Corner chimneys kept temperature constant as the worms devoured the mulberry leaves and spun their valuable cocoons on fan-like branches of cut heather. The 'bread tree' had been succeeded by a 'gold tree' people said, and houses, landscape and lifestyles showed the difference.

LIMOUSIN

The wooded Limousin hills sustained a polyculture that in the 19th century changed to sheep, then cattle. A land of granite and schist, trees and water, many peasants depended on chestnuts for their 'bread' and emigration was widespread. Seasonal jobs were regularly taken elsewhere in winter and Creuse stone masons were in demand as far away as Paris.

Most Limousin farmhouses date from the late 19th century – it is estimated that only one in three is older than 100 years – and there is considerable diversity.

But it is due to the writings of Pierre Deffontaines, who sought to delineate regional house styles in the 1930s, that a particular type of house comes to be called 'Limousin'. It is a form of longhouse similar to types found throughout the west and, in Limousin, its home is largely the Millevaches plateau. Usually its construction predates 1870.

Low, one-storeyed with a stable attached, the house is built of granite or schist bound with clay mortar, the corner stones are dressed and the lintels made of wood or stone. Small windows are traditional though few original windows remain; the shutters are often pierced with a lozenge or heart motif. Invariably the stable entrance is in the facade and there is often a break in the roof ridge to indicate the point of separation between dwelling and stable. Roofs are either two- or four-sloped. Until 1850 half of Limousin houses were covered with thatch but on the plateau slates have become customary and in other areas *lauzes* and tiles are common.

A barn-cum-stable found in southern Limousin and north Dordogne is of special interest. Called a *grange chapiteau* it harks back to a very early form of building, when corners still presented something of a challenge. The barn is oval shaped, its low schist walls bound with clay mortar. Though between 15 to 30 metres long and eight to 15 metres wide, the barn's height is *always* 12 metres – the huge thatched roof giving the building its extraordinary 'capped' appearance. A double door on the long side flanked by smaller ones reflects the central aisle arrangement common to *granges-étables*. An 18th century survey showed some 2000 of these barns in existence, but sadly only a handful remain today, all but one of them covered in corrugated tin.

Above: rare oval-shaped barn: grange chapiteau.

Right: Limousin longhouse on the Millevaches plateau.

LOIRE VALLEY

Above left: cream-coloured tufa cut into ashlar is typical of the Touraine.

Though several farmhouse styles exist, the Loire valley farmhouse probably finds its best expression around Saumur and Tours. Two significant factors contributed to its success. The first was the availability of a soft limestone or tufa which, easily carved and of high quality, did not when properly seasoned need rendering to protect it from the elements. The exquisitely pale champagne hue, bound with an equally fine lime mortar, is extremely elegant and appealing.

The second factor is historical. In the 15th century the Loire's game-stocked forests and beautiful scenery repeatedly drew king and court from Paris, and the magnificent chateaux erected by them on the Loire became the talk of Europe. Who locally could resist this heady influence? There was now an abundance of skilled craftsmen in the region, and it was prosperous. Before long even the simplest houses were being built of dressed tufa and decorated with fine cornices and elegantly carved dormers inspired by those of Renaissance chateaux. Even the many troglodyte houses in natural caves and former quarries along the river bank have dressed tufa facades like ordinary houses.

Disappearing Baugé roof.

Covered gable stair.

Before long quality slate from Anjou, used on chateau roofs, began to replace the peasants' humble thatch, but the steep roof pitch and gable parapets designed to protect the thatch remained. Farmhouses also kept their split 'stable' doors: the top half left open for light and air also helped the chimney to draw. But in the 19th century glass-paned transoms began to be installed. Pigstys and ovens were attached to gables (the seigneurial ban on ovens having lapsed here as early as the 17th century), and an exterior gable stair, often roofed, was also added.

A unique if eclectic roofing style is found around Baugé. Here canal tiles have a hook on the back, like flat tiles, to attach them to the roof battens. And instead of covering the joins with convex tiles a strip of lime mortar was applied. Not many *baugé*-covered dwellings remain today but quite a few outbuildings can be seen roofed in this fashion.

LORRAINE

Though regularly linked to Alsace, Lorraine differs markedly from its Germanic neighbour and nowhere is this more evident than in architecture. In both provinces the population is grouped in villages but Lorraine villages are most unusual. Though individually built, each house is joined to its neighbours in a row along what is usually the only village street. Set back three or four metres from the street the front yards form a sort of common court *(usoir* or *parge)*. Here farm carts were parked and the family dunghill rose, its dimensions the well-known measure of a daughter's dowry; while behind the curtain wall of uniformly dull grey houses, orchards and meadows spread like so many secret gardens.

There are other surprises too – most famously, Mediterranean style roofs. The strange anomaly of canal tiles so far north is explained by the longtime presence of Rome's eighth legion in Lorraine and, in addition to canal tiles, a few Roman-style roofs with flat lower tiles *(imbrex)* can still be found in the Meuse department, *e.g.* at Tronville.

Another extraordinary feature is that, though joined, each house is much deeper than it is wide; some going back as much as 30 or 40 metres

Maison bloc's *three doors serve dwelling, stable and carthouse respectively.*

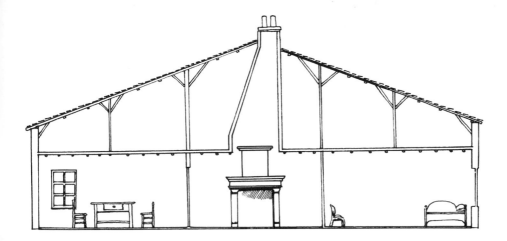

Transverse section of dwelling showing central chimney and below it a windowless kitchen with wall-mounted fireplace, a later addition.

– the dwelling, barn and stable set perpendicular to the facade, as shown. The big double barn doors are often arched, adding a touch of elegance to the otherwise sombre facades.

The living area comprises three rooms, one *behind* the other: the sitting room *(poêle)* is on the street and behind it is the kitchen, followed by a bedroom at the back. A narrow corridor alongside connects the rooms, or else entry is through the barn. But either way it means the kitchen is hemmed in without any windows. At first this was not a problem because the stone-floored kitchen is shaped like a gigantic funnel. The opening at the top of the 'funnel' emitted smoke but it also let in plenty of light, the conduit acting as a smokehouse for meat hanging in the upper regions. (see Franche-Comté for details).

In the 19th century however it became fashionable to install a conventional fireplace against the kitchen wall, its flue running up one side of the 'funnel'. The overhead void was then glazed at ceiling level to make a lightwell, or *flammande.* But memories are short and inhabitants gleefully explain the whole thing as a way of avoiding window tax.

To achieve the houses' unusual depth, Lorraine builders employed two different roof structures: the ancient aisled hall technique (see Roofs) created the necessary depth, but was slightly awkward because the aisles ran parallel to the ridgeline and Lorraine interiors are perpendicular to it. The second technique solved this problem by employing posts either built into the dividing walls or set on them, to support the purlins overhead.

Unlike the rest of Lorraine, houses in the Vosges hills are dispersed about the countryside. Typical mountain chalets, a closer look reveals a tendency for depth over width, proclaiming their Lorraine parentage. Often two-storeyed and made of granite, the weatherboarded gables helped air crops stored in the copious lofts. And as with so many mountain dwellings, the hillside was regularly used for access, via a ramp, directly into the loft.

LYONNAIS

Comprising most of the departments of Rhône, Loire and Ain, Lyonnais architecture is diverse but two styles are of particular note: the high-houses of wine-growers' and the delightful half-timbered houses of southern Bresse, famous for their spectacular chimney stacks.

Before the late 19th century grapes were grown throughout the Lyonnais and high-houses can be found dotted across the entire region, their ground floors well-appointed for storing heavy barrels and vats. But stylistic details vary in each locality, making the area an excellent one in which to study high-house diversity (more so if next door Burgundy is included).

Today wine-growing is largely confined to Beaujolais where houses are usually of stone, and sometimes *pisé*. The roofs are hipped and very often the ground floor *cave* is partially dug out – a gesture to northern habits in this largely canal-tiled region.

Nearby in the low-lying Tarare mountains an elegant variation on the high-house theme is found: a stone pillared gallery, probably Italian inspired, runs the length of the house making a graceful first-floor loggia. While in the southeast, in Bugey, stepped gables attest the earlier tradition of thatch.

Beaujolais winegrowers' houses grouped in this instance round a communal court.

Bresse verandas and balconies evolved for drying maize. This house at St Trivier-de-Courtes, with a Saracen chimney-stack, is open to the public.

Bresse houses on the other hand are long and low, with lodging on the ground floor. Half-timbered or of *pisé,* the roof extends forward to create a delightful veranda spanning the long facade. A wooden staircase underneath leads to the balcony and granary above. Both the veranda and balcony were introduced early in the 18th century together with maize as a means of drying it – a good example of structural adaptation to meet agrarian needs. The result is a very comfortable house – among the most charming in France – and fat bundles of maize still hang from verandas in colourful tribute to their *raison d'être.*

Bresse houses also pinpoint the border between northern and southern France. Northern Bresse (Bresse Louhannaise) is part of Burgundy and its houses have steep roofs in the Germanic style, covered with flat tiles. But this gives way quite rapidly to weak slopes and canal tiles in southern Bresse (Bresse Savoyarde). In other respects the houses are very much alike.

But it is the chimney stack, called Saracen, that has made Bresse architecture famous, and it is found almost entirely in Bresse Savoyarde.

As in Franche-Comté, Lorraine and Savoy traditional Bresse chimneys are huge funnels in the kitchen ceiling. The cooking was done on a central hearth beneath. Chimneys of this sort (described in detail under Franche-Comté) were known in northern Europe in Celtic times. In Bresse they are half-timbered constructions supported on one side by the wall and on the other by a two foot thick beam stretching the width of the house. The square chimney opening some four metres wide is an impressive affair; but it is the chimney's *stack* that is unique. Rising three to five metres above the roof it is built of lime-plastered brick. A mitre

Close up of a Saracen chimney-stack.

169

shape – round, square or octagonal at base – the stack is crowned by a monumental decoration utterly foreign to peasant architecture.

The origins of this eccentric and elegant structure is something of a mystery. The minaret appearance of some suggests, like the name Saracen, an oriental root; but other examples have a gothic flavour. There were reputedly numerous such chimneys in the Middle Ages, of which only 31 remain today, the oldest dating from the 17th century. And scholars now believe they were inspired by local religious architecture, 'saracen' being a word used to describe anything that was foreign or bizarre.

Curiously the stacks are all on land once held by the sires of Bagé, whose power was at its height between the 10th and 13th century. But why peasants (or their masters) should have expended their resources on such finery remains unanswered.

Charming Bresse farmhouse showing mix of materials used to great advantage in stone-free areas: in this case half-timbering with brick infill; also pisé *in* banchage *construction.*

MIDI-PYRENEES

Midi-Pyrénées is limited here to the regions surrounding Toulouse and Montauban – part of lower Quercy – and the Pyrénées Ariège. It contains some of the most beautiful brick houses in France.

Roman influence was very strong in and around Toulouse and it was no coincidence that the medieval revival of brickmaking found a major centre here. The word *'teule'* is Occitan and meant both brick and tile, the two being virtually indistinguishable. The spread of bastides in the 13th century gave brick an added impetus, enlarged in the 15th and 16th centuries by local prosperity derived from the Toulouse woad trade. (Woad produced an indigo-like blue dye.) Despite the expense of firing bricks, many could now afford to do so and the tradition established itself.

A region of polyculture, maize and market gardening it is the market gardener's house to the north and west of the city that best typifies the Toulouse area today. One-storeyed brick – or brick and pebbles or adobe – most of these houses were built in the late 19th century. Their elegant symmetrical facades are capped by overhanging canal-tiled roofs and, unlike other forms of *maison bloc,* the dwelling is at the centre of the

*Beautifully
proportioned all brick
'master's house' outside
Toulouse.*

building, flanked by outbuildings on the ends. These generally include an open hangar supported by square brick pillars.

There are also many 'masters' houses' or *maisons de maître* around Toulouse. Two-storeyed and square, they too are built of brick or brick and pebbles, and are topped by a hipped roof. But their outbuildings are separate, and quite often are made of adobe.

A number of houses, both *maisons de maître* and local farmhouses, have rendered exteriors with brick only in evidence as trim round the windows and doors.

Maison bloc brick houses are also found in the Lauragais hills to the southeast of Toulouse. Built on hilltops, their scale and position have from afar the aspect of ancient monasteries. Some are of really extraordinary length and many use the arch to great effect. Brick is of course well-suited to arch construction and a few farmsteads have brick arcades spanning the entire facade.

*This elegant shell pink
facade, probably adobe
underneath, is
brilliantly relieved by
traditional red brick
trim and tiny* jours.

LOWER QUERCY After the Revolution several Quercy cantons were ceded to the department of Tarn and Garonne and the very appealing farmhouses in this area are typical of the middle Garonne: squarish, they are constructed of white limestone or of brick or adobe, with hipped canal-tiled roofs. Dovecotes are very frequent (true of most of the region), especially the one-sloped *à casquette* style; and a number of dovecotes have terracotta pigeons mounted on them to attract the live birds.

Adobe dovecote with crumbling mud rendering; the top half was for pigeons and the bottom used as a store.

To the south, the **PYRENEES ARIEGEOISES** is a country of grey granite, snow-capped peaks and apple-blossom in the spring. As in the Alps the custom of transhumance prevailed and some villages in the high mountains were inhabited only during the summer months.

High-house architecture is dominant here and houses are characterised by a narrow balcony some 18 inches wide recessed in the facade. The steeply slanted roofs, originally thatched, are clad with fishtail slates and in the villages many older houses possess south-facing loggias and galleries.

Stepped granite gables are sometimes seen on barns (at Cominac the thatch also survives, as it does on several houses around Salsein). Stepped gables helped to protect thatch and keep it in place and the 'stepping stones' were handy for putting out fires and cleaning chimneys.

Dry-stone huts called *orries* were also part of mountain life. Made of encorbelled stones with a layer of turf on one side to protect them from the wind, *orries* are rounded outside and squarish within and bear a strong resemblance to neolithic forts. Both had among other similarities niches in the walls for belongings – in *orries* there is also one for the dog. A few *orries* are in fact a complex of buildings, part shepherds' lodgings, part dairies and cheese stores.

Recessed balcony in the Pyrénées Ariège.

NORMANDY

Geography splits Normandy neatly into two, and with it architecture. Lower Normandy, part of the ancient Armorican Massif, possesses enormous quantities of stone: a bedrock of granite, sandstone and schist underpins the peninsula, giving way further east to high-quality limestone on the plain of Caen. But in upper Normandy chalk predominates, hidden under a blanket of alluvial clay; and in the absence of a more durable stone the clay was put to use by builders. Combined with timber framing – often the work of shipyard carpenters from the Seine valley – the marriage produced some of the country's finest vernacular buildings.

UPPER NORMANDY In the oldest half-timbered houses verticality is what strikes the eye. The smaller timbers *(potelets)* are regularly and simply spaced, sometimes close together sometimes far apart, in a row of regimented stripes and unspoilt upright lines. The corner posts accent this, running the full height of the building. But a shortage of big timbers

Black and white Norman farmhouse with one-sloped dormers, ladder stair and classic double windows has been tastefully restored.

soon caused the introduction of horizontal elements. Horizontal beams or stringers enabled shorter timbers to be used both as corner posts and *potelets*. It also opened up a realm of timber pattern-making that reached its full elaboration in the 18th century. At first obliquely set *potelets* were only used at corners to steady the overall structure but soon highly decorative criss-crosses, chevrons and lozenges appeared, especially on the upper facade where the timbers were protected by overhanging eaves.

Typically these houses are one-storeyed, long and rather narrow; their capacious four-sloped roofs broken by a row of dormers *à la capucine* (three-sloped). Many had a pulley to lift up crops for storage. An external stair along the gable, protected by a hooded extension of the roof, combined to produce a uniquely Norman silhouette.

Early roofs were covered in thatch *(chaume),* which is why farmhouses are so often called *chaumières,* though their thatch has long since been replaced by slates – or a cladding of flat rosy tiles. Where thatch remains however or has been put back (as in the Marais Vernier), a row of yellow irises bloom along the ridge, absorbing the damp and hinting at forgotten magical formulae.

Windows too have a special look. Though most date from the 19th century their appearance is somewhat earlier. Each panel contains not one but *two* rows of small panes and often two windows are set side by side, divided by a structural post, so that the overall effect is square or horizontal. Shutters of plain planks are removable or, hinged in the centre, fold back against the wall.

Two or three rooms, each with an *exterior* door, was customary. Nor was it unusual to find a stable or cartshed on the end of a house, but rarely more. Half-timbered additions are hard to build and fire was a serious threat under thatch; so outbuildings were scattered. Often they included a cider mill housed in a rectangular building, the apple store overhead entered by an exterior stair (see Outbuildings).

Dovecotes, especially prevalent in Caux, were exclusive to seigneurial domains, and are elegantly constructed: brick, black and white flint and/or limestone are deployed in various geometric patterns.

CAUX, set on a broad and rolling plain, supports a special type of farmstead. Called a *clos masure* the house, outbuildings, pond and apple orchard are enclosed by a rectangular earthen bank *(talus)* crowned by a row of trees. Acting as a fence and windbreak the trees also supplied wood for cabinetmaking and repairs. Formerly oak and elm these have been superseded by beech. In winter cows were kept inside the earthen-walled compound, as in the Iron Age forts this plan so strongly resembles.

Cauchoise houses have crosses and lozenge motifs in abundance

Normandy gable stair.

175

above the middle stringer, but below it timbers are strictly vertical. But clay and wood are not the only materials used: many houses are made of flint with brick trim and only the outbuildings are *colombage*.

LOWER NORMANDY Farmhouses in the Cotentin peninsula are similar to houses in Brittany. Built of granite and schist with imposing chimneys at each end, their roofs – once thatched or covered in schist – are today largely under slate. Dormers are fewer than elsewhere: sometimes only one, accessible by a ladder; and buildings tend to be grouped around an open court – an arrangement well-suited to the non-specialized mode of farming prevalent in the *bocage*. But floor plans, even of richer houses, keep the two room plan of simple dwellings.

To the east, the limestone plain of Caen and the Bessin were enormously prosperous. Farmsteads are large and are enclosed in courts entered by a covered gateway. The most imposing building is usually the barn: finely built it comprises two floors and a loft with an exterior stone stair (see page 89).

Cows and a glimpse of zebra-striped half-timbering epitomize the upper Normandy landscape. Note the stone-built ground floor.

Left: elegant manor-style farmhouse in the Eure.

Below: traditional life continues in this thatched longhouse in the Marais Vernier, its loft burgeoning with hay.

PERIGORD

Once awash with seigneurs, their chateaux and manors have long attracted attention in Périgord: there are over 1000 of them, an average of two per canton. Farmhouse architecture is a more recent discovery and it is surprisingly varied. Devastated by wars and famines the province was frequently repopulated and this is evident in local building styles.

Yet one particular type of house is representative. Its chief locale is Périgord Noir and its most salient feature is the roof: steep and flat-tiled it can measure up to two-thirds of a dwelling's total height. It is the more remarkable for existing in a traditionally canal-tiled zone.

Most typically, Périgourdine roofs have four slopes, a pronounced *coyau* and are covered in russet brown tiles. But in Sarladais there still exist magnificent *lauze* roofs made of limestone plaques. Paradoxically canal-tiled cornices (*génoises*) are also seen, their depth – one to three rows – reflecting the house's importance.

A classic Périgordine roof rises above ripening vineyards.

Dormers and small triangular *houteaux* (rare in other parts of the country) give ventilation to the loft. And in the Sarladais elegantly carved shell and scroll designs on dormers shows the influence chateau architecture had on wealthier farmers.

Most often houses are one-storeyed with small windows and a door made of a single batten; a three-paned transom is set overhead. The houses are built of limestone, the colour and quality varying in different places. Around Riberac it is a creamy white and has given its name to the area: Périgord Blanc; while in Périgord Noir a warm, honey-gold colour is indigenous, similar to that in the English Cotswolds.

Inside houses a stair along the kitchen wall is sealed at the third step by a door and the large fireplace — either recessed, with huge flat flanking stones, or else supported on corbels — is called *a cantou,* a reference in Occitan to the settles placed on either side. There is usually a *chai* at the back of the house for storing wine.

Although both terracotta and wood were customary for flooring some older houses have pebble mosaic floors — a reminder that Périgord was once called Petrocori. Known as *pichadis* the pebbles are set in arcane geometric patterns and embedded in *pisé.*

Dovecotes are frequent in Périgord where they had seigneurial associations. There are, too, numerous *gariottes,* as their dry-stone cabins are called. Used as toolsheds or shepherds huts these were often quickly constructed using stones collected in the fields. Some wellheads were built in a similar fashion using mortar.

Left: scroll-fronted dormers are a feature of Périgord Noir.

Above: flat-tiled roof of farmhouse near Bergerac is much taller than the lodging.

POITOU-CHARENTES

Poitou-Charentes houses are often labelled 'transitional', suggesting outside influences instead of development from within. And in a region of *bocage,* plains, marsh and seacoast – where many different needs must be met – borrowing was a good solution. Nevertheless a distinctly 'Poitou-Charentes' house exists, and can be instantly recognized as such.

Long, narrow, one-and-a-half storeyed and roofed in canal tiles, it comprises two rooms. The stable may be attached or separate. Built of rubble limestone or in certain areas schist, its windows, doors and corners are framed with dressed stones. The facade is rendered and painted white, though the other walls are not. Square or bulls-eye shaped *jours* ventilate the loft and a bulls-eye *jour* is also found above the kitchen sink.

The spruced-up facades of houses can make it more interesting to approach villages from behind, encountering a jumble of mellow, exposed stone walls infinitely more suggestive of the past than the facades, which can look quite recent. In fact the majority of houses are 19th century and many that are older have a one-sloped roof, known locally as *'cul levé'*.

Symmetry, a characteristic of local facades, is greatly enhanced by the use of jours, *small windows that ventilate the loft.*

Above: simplicity and prosperity are combined in one of the many 'masters' houses' found throughout Poitou-Charentes.

Left: charming maison basse *with open hayloft in the Marais Poitevin.*

But there are several variations of the basic form. For example Poitou houses have interconnecting rooms while a central corridor is usual in Charente – the sink located in it next to the front door. Hipped roofs are more common in Charente than Poitou, and in Aunis, Bas Poitou and north Saintonge a half-hip is found at one end – the west, which is the most exposed to wind.

One of the the prettiest variations is in the Poitevin marshlands (Marais Poitevin). This enchanting region, known as '*Venise verte*', is now a national park and gliding along the quiet waters of its canals, low-lying, whitewashed houses appear on either side adorned with vividly painted shutters. A loggia-like hayloft opens above the stable on one side and a flat-bottomed boat is moored at the bottom of the garden. The farmers transport cattle in them.

Around Cognac and the central plain of Poitou are numerous *maisons de maître* built by prosperous farmers and wine-growers. Consisting of two or four rooms divided by a corridor, with bedrooms upstairs and a *chai* in the court, one sub-type makes local priorities quite clear: the large *salle* gives directly on to a *chai* at the back and, almost an afterthought, the other rooms are reached by a separate door in the facade. Many farmsteads are grouped in villages. Set in enclosed courtyards their monumental gateways form a double arch: the big double door for vehicles flanked by a smaller one for those on foot.

An imposing three-aisled barn is also noteworthy. Developed in response to changing agricultural needs, two wings flank the central aisle, creating an ecclesiastical shape. Carts were housed in the 'nave' and animals in the wings separated from the central aisle by a long wall.

PROVENCE

Villages are the main habitat in Provence. Perched for protection on hilltops or steep mountain slopes (only much later did they appear on the plains) space was at a premium and buildings grew upwards, not outwards, squashed into narrow winding streets. The ground floors sheltered animals and stores, though sheepfolds and temporary lodgings were often built outside villages nearer to the fields.

In the countryside buildings could develop laterally, sprawling in long rectangles as annexes were added, usually at different heights to that

of the main roof. The resulting 'agglomerated' style is a prime characteristic of the Provençal *mas,* or farmhouse. Dovecotes are another, their roofs frequently one-sloped in the southern style (see Outbuildings). Those attached to houses either flank one side or jut importantly above the roof line, turret-like.

Most houses are built of rubble limestone (pebbles and clay in the Durance valley and Camargue) and exteriors are rendered in a rough or smooth texture, depending on whether a thyme brush was used or extra sand added to the final coat.

But it is colour that creates the strongest impression in Provence. A palette of subtle and delicate hues – rose, ochre, sable, beige, cream and lavender – produced by oxides in the local sand embellishes what are otherwise plain facades. Shutters are painted to contrast in faded cerulean blues, mossy greens or browns and, together with canal-tiled roofs, exude a decidedly Mediterranean flavour.

Roofs are emphasized by canal-tiled cornices *(génoises).* Provençal *génoises* lack the bands of flat tiles normally found between the canal tile rows and they are not confined to eaves. They turn corners and ascend gables to create pediments suggestive of the region's classical past – Provence was Roman-occupied Provincia.

But plaster and lath cornices are also seen. Rare outside Ile de France, plaster of Paris was regularly used in Provence as mortar and as interior and exterior plaster, especially around Digne where it maintains its attractive rosy-ochre hue.

In front of houses a terrace shaded by an overhead trellis makes a summer drawing-room. Further shade comes from plane or mulberry trees and, behind the house, a screen of cypresses protects against the northerly mistral blasts.

With the exception of village dwellings (and high-houses in the Durance valley), kitchens are customarily on the ground floor, separated from store rooms and cellar by a corridor. Two types of fireplace are common: 'provençal', having a low hearth under a great hood and 'Marseille' which has a raised platform hearth ('demi-Marseille' being only slightly raised). Provençal floors are tiled with small often hexagonal-shaped tiles called *tomettes*.

Another fixture is a terracotta wash tub embedded in the kitchen wall or a niche with shelves that could be reassembled vertically into a container (though in the Vaucluse and Rhône valley a small room off the kitchen was used for washing).

Provençal terms can be confusing. Though *mas* generally denotes a farmhouse (the word is singular and plural), in the Camargue and Crau it

Dry-stone borie *is one in a village of similar constructions located in the Vaucluse.*

Opposite: the village of Gordes, built on a hilltop for protection.

*Above: ochre and blue
farmhouse beautifully
illustrates the warm
and earthy colours that
give Provençal houses
much of their character.*

*Right: wisteria-clad
verandas are the
region's summer
drawingrooms.*

means a large-holding where the house, of imposing dimensions and built of dressed stone, lodged both master and steward. Older Camargue and Crau *mas* sometimes occupy the sites of former Roman villas. *Caves,* sheds, store rooms and dovecote are attached in a long rectangular agglomeration; and the nearby sheepfold could house up to a thousand head.

Shepherds and workmen in the Camargue inhabited picturesque huts known as *cabanes de gardian.* These chapel-like dwellings have an apse at one end and are made of reeds and cob with a stone gable. They were divided into two rooms by a reed partition.

Ostau is another word for farmhouse but most usually it refers to a multi-storeyed dwelling in a village.

Bastide on the other hand denotes a gentleman's house of the type found around Aix and Marseilles. Often summer residences *bastides* lack agricultural annexes and a number of very old ones have corner towers, blending indistinguishably with chateaux. Normally built in a bourgeois style, *i.e.* square with hipped roofs, louvred shutters and symmetrical facades, *bastides* were surrounded by the appurtenances of leisured country life; their carefully laid out gardens and well-kept lawns differing greatly from peasant houses organized around work. (To complicate matters, in upper Provence *bastide* can mean a mountain dwelling while in southwest France it is a 13th century town built around a central square.)

There are too the famous *bories* of the Vaucluse. These remarkable limestone huts assembled without mortar or roof carpentry were dwellings, sheep pens and/or storage sheds. Comprising one or two storeys some are organized around a walled courtyard, with ovens, chimneys and niches for storage inside their thickly built dry-stone walls. Though none extant predates the 17th century evidence points to a tradition at least as old as the Iron Age.

Camargue shepherd's cabin.

Camargue mas *of Pont de Rousty, built in 1850, has lodging in centre flanked by cowhouse/barn and traditional one-sloped dovecote.*

185

QUERCY

The Quercy farmhouse epitomizes high-house architecture and, at its best, is among the most elegant of this type in France.

Typically an exterior stone stair leads to an upstairs veranda which is usually, but not always, covered by a roof supported on wood, stone or brick posts. The roof can be an extension of the main roof or a separate projection but in either case the veranda is called a *bolet,* and the house a *'maison à bolet'.* In a number of more prosperous houses the *bolet* extends across the entire facade.

But though a classic form of high-house, several features have evolved to suit local needs. For example a stone sink or *évier* is often found in the *bolet* wall, useful for domestic tasks like peeling potatoes and plucking chickens performed in the *bolet's* cooling shade.

On the ground floor the *cave* is sometimes vaulted and under the exterior stair is the pigsty or a grain store, its door and the one above it arched attractively.

Roofs vary: either they are a steep Périgourdine style with flat tiles (*lauzes* and fishtail slates in the east) or, as in lower Quercy, shallow sloped and canal tiled.

Quercy stone varies in quality and colour: an appealing pale ochre of good quality is found in the east around La Capelle Marival, and a beautiful white limestone in lower Quercy (see also Midi-Pyrénées).

One of the prettiest features of Quercy houses is the *souillarde* or pantry. An alcove off the kitchen it is handsomely rounded like an apsidal chapel. A stone sink is embedded in the wall and a carved stone shelf for pots and pans belts the alcove like a dado. Nowadays this little room is usually the 'office'.

Traditionally fireplaces are in the gable and, as in Périgord, have a settle on either side.

After high-houses dovecotes are the region's dominant architectural feature, and very often the two are combined. Dovecotes were never exclusive to the nobility in Quercy – who were only five per cent of its population – and there is accommodation for pigeons on virtually every farm. South of the Lot river these tend to be pigeonholes in the walls of houses but elsewhere dovecotes are usually attached to the house, flanking the facade or protruding elegantly from the roof in mimicry of chateaux. In the Segala they straddle the front of barn roofs like church steeples.

Freestanding dovecotes are rare and roofs are generally four-sloped or the slanted, one-sloped style popular throughout the south. In lower Quercy are a few dovecotes on columns, a form borrowed from Agenais neighbours (see also Outbuildings).

Above: pantry (souillarde) in apse-shaped alcove.

Above and opposite: dovecotes flank two elegant high-houses in the Lot south of Cahors.

Today, Vendée cottages (bourinnes) *are mostly roofed in canal-tiles, their white facades highlighted by bright boat-coloured shutters and doors.*

VENDEE

A local word used to describe a particular type of dwelling often suggests a local origin, and the *bourinne* is peculiar to the Vendée. Found in the coastal marshlands (Marais Breton-Vendée) it was made entirely of plant material. Constructed of clay and roofed with reed or bulrushes (though canal tiles are seen today), *bourinnes* housed the very poor and were often hastily built – at least to begin with.

Ancient custom allowed any building with a smoking chimney to stay where it was, so *bourinnes* would spring up overnight along the dykes, like mushrooms. Once the right to existence had been established a more solid version could be built. This was done using the *bauge* method. Great lumps of clay *(bigots)* were hoisted on to walls with a pitchfork one row at a time. Eight days were needed for drying before the next row of *bigots* could be added. Begun in the spring, a dwelling was ready for its occupants by autumn.

Bourinne walls can be very thick, some of them measuring up to two metres. Chimneys too are made of clay and were hand-modelled, as was the bread oven attached to the chimney. The oven dome was achieved by the ancient method of filling the void with sand until the shape was dry.

Whitewashed inside and out, shutters are painted blue or green – boat colours. There is no loft.

Today the word *bourinne* is losing its specific attribution and becoming synonyous with cottage, as is *'penty'* in lower Brittany.

Thatched bourinne *with short clay chimney stack and few windows is a fine example of the traditional style.*

APPENDIX

MORTARS PLASTERS & LIMEWASH

Modern cement should never be used in restoration work except for foundations below ground where a dry, non-porous seal is required. Cement and hydraulic lime plasters and mortars keep walls from breathing and damp becomes trapped inside. Vinyl emulsion paint does this as well. For stone or brick walls therefore slaked lime *(chaux grasse)* is recommended.

Slaked lime can be bought in putty form or, as quicklime, it can be slaked at home. Factory-produced slaked lime is available in 50 kilo sacks. The product, AFNOR 15-510: *chaux aérienne éteinte pour le bâtiment* or CAEB, is able to absorb sand colour so that colours natural to the region can be successfully produced. CAEB is sometimes known as *'fleur de chaux'.*

For local sources of CAEB write to Maisons Paysannes de France, 32 rue Pierre Semard, 75009 Paris.

The Lime Centre, Long Barn, Morestead, Winchester, Hampshire offers short courses in the traditional uses of lime and will also match shades of lime mortar and limewash.

SLAKING LIME Always remember that lime is highly caustic and hands and clothing must be properly protected. Quicklime *(chaux vive)* is particularly dangerous to eyes, and goggles should be worn when slaking it.

The putty produced from home-slaked lime can be kept indefinitely in airtight buckets under a few mm of water and it will improve with age. (This also applies to mortar but it must be kneaded again before use.) Putty is usable 24 hours after mixing but a minimum of three months is recommended.

To slake lime secure a metal rust-proof bucket by placing stones or bricks around it. Fill bucket half full with clean water and add a pint of quicklime. *Never begin by adding water to quicklime, this can be very dangerous.* NB: if limewash for an exterior surface is being made add a lemon-sized lump of tallow, shredded, to the water before adding the quicklime.

The mixture will boil like a witch's cauldron (and the tallow dissolves in the process).

Stir the mixture with a long-handled paddle to dislodge any settled bits. If it is too thick to stir, add a little more water. When all is quiet and thoroughly mixed, cover the bucket securely and leave to cool.

LIME PLASTER *(enduit or crépi)*
White: 3 parts yellow sand, 1 part slaked lime, 1 part linseed oil.
Brown tinted: 4 parts red sand to one part each of clay soil, slaked lime, linseed oil and animal hair.

To use: the first coat *(gobetis)* is put on roughly with a trowel. Three or four coats may be put on in this manner or by machine, but to give a hand-finished look the final coat should ideally be applied with a *'taloche'* (a wood float) or a brush *'mouchetis'*. The plaster should be no more than 1cm thick or fissures will be likely to appear.

Sometimes the final coat is lime and sand but no clay, and this makes a more impermeable surface.

To plaster over *torchis* or *pisé* the walls must first be pitted with a Scotch hammer or similar object to help adhesion. Builders used to use a pitchfork.

WHITE LIME MORTAR is suitable for fine joints.
Mix to a stiff consistency 1 part slaked lime, sieved, to to 1 part silver sand. Add 2 litres boiled linseed oil per M3 lime/sand mixture and work to a fine paste.

Traditionally linseed oil was also used to prime surfaces before applying mortar.

LIMEWASH A bucket of limewash will cover the walls and ceiling of an average room. More precisely, 1 litre = 6 sq metres. But since limewash is translucent several coats will be required, especially out of doors. Limewash can be made from CAEB or from home-slaked lime. The latter gives better results but is more difficult to work. These instructions are for both types. (Limewash can also be purchased in several shades from Papers and Paints Ltd, 4 Park Walk, London, SW10 OAD or matched at the Lime Centre — see above)

To make limewash: place about three trowelfuls of lime putty in a bucket with a few inches of water and, using the whisk, make a smooth paste. Keep adding water and whisking until the mixture is like a thin cream. (If your home-made quicklime is already milky omit this step.)

If the wash is to be used externally, half a cup of raw linseed oil can be added.

Sieve the mixture into second bucket, then stir in any pigment.

Dilute the mixture until it is the consistency of milk and sieve back into the first bucket.

To use: apply thinly in three or more coats to a clean surface. It is important to moisten the surface well as you go, spraying about 4 square yards at a time so that the walls will not suck the limewash in too quickly. Leave at least 24 hours between coats and dampen down the surface before each coat is applied.

PLASTER OF PARIS To obtain a finish similar to traditional exterior plaster mix 40kg of fine plaster with 6kg of slaked lime *(chaux grasse)* and 20kg of river sand.

Before applying the mixture the old surface must be roughened and a bastard lime mortar (a mixture of slaked and hydraulic lime) applied to help bind the mixture to the old surface. Alternatively a ceramic trellis is sometimes nailed to the structure.

TORCHIS

To make torchis mix $^1/2$ bucket of water to 12 buckets of soil (roughly 40% silt and 20% clay) which may itself be mixed with a little lime or dung. Then add 12 buckets of sand.

Tread soil, adding handfuls of chopped straw and tread again: you cannot over mix but it is easier to mix small batches at a time.

To apply: spray 'trellis' with water and apply *torchis* to both sides, beginning at the bottom. Press firmly into place with hands or trowel and finally smooth with a wood float. The coat should be some 12 to 30mm thick.

A panel of *torchis* can take some two weeks to dry and should be checked regularly for cracks. Covering with damp sacking assists even drying.

Torchis is normally rendered with lime plaster *(enduit)* as described above.

PISE

It is said that where a stream has vertical banks the soil is usually good for *pisé,* a semi-dry mixture, ideally 25-30% clay and 70-75% sand and gravel — in other words a type of soil known as sandy loam. *Pisé's* water content is estimated at 10% in sandy soil and 20% in clayey soil.

To test, squeeze a ball of soil the size of an egg, hold at arm's length and drop it on hard ground. If it shatters into its former loose state then it is about right.

ADOBE

A mixture of at least 50% sand, 5-15% clay, 16-20% water and a little chopped straw.

Dug clay was exposed to winter frosts then mixed with straw, trodden and turned to make a sticky mass that could be picked up with a fork.

Moulds without top or bottom were wetted or oiled — some were metal-lined— to make it easier to remove bricks. The clay mixture was packed in and smoothed with a wire bow, then the mould was removed to form the next block. After sun-drying for 2 or 3 days, the bricks were dried again in openwork stacking.

TERRACOTTA TILES

The old method of laying tiles is no longer viable and a bastard mortar of lime and cement can be used or a membrane of plastic or other material laid beneath the tiles. The tiles should be laid as closely together as possible — wide joints are a modern fashion — and the joints should be filled with lime mortar. Cement mortar turns terracotta grey.

Before laying, both old and new terracotta tiles must be soaked in water for 24 hours. After laying, the tiles should be cleaned by drenching them with diesel fuel. Then apply two coats of a mixture 2/3 linseed oil to 1/3 turpentine, leaving 24 hours in between coats; after which the tiles can be waxed.

Old tiles can often be purchased from demolition companies and some *tuileries* make hand-finished tiles that mimic old ones reasonably well.

GENERAL INFORMATION

Maisons Paysannes de France 32 rue Pierre Semard, 75009 Paris is a non-profit making organisation dedicated to the preservation of old farmhouses. They can supply information about local sources of traditional building materials and each *département* has a representative who can give advice about local traditions and materials. Members receive a regular newsletter and the organisation publishes a number of pamphlets on regional styles and effective restoration schemes. English is spoken.

BIBLIOGRAPHY

Note: where translations exist the English publication is given.

GENERAL AND SOCIAL HISTORY

Ardagh, J: **Rural France**, *London 1983*

Bloc M: **French Rural History**, *Berkeley 1966*

Braudel, F: **The Identity of France**, 2 vols, *London 1990*

Cole, R: **A Traveller's History of France**, *London 1988*

Duby, G (ed.): **Histoire de la France rurale**, 3 vols, *Paris 1975*

Goubert, P: **The French Peasantry in the Seventeenth Century**, *Cambridge 1986*

Ladurie, E Le Roy: **The French Peasantry 1450-1660**, *London 1987*

Ladurie, E Le Roy: **Montaillou**, *London 1978*

Lough, J: **Introduction to Seventeenth Century France**, *London 1954*

Moulin, A: **Peasantry and Society in France since 1789**, *London 1991*

Price, R: **A Social History of 19th Century France**, *London 1987*

Segalen, M: **Love and Power in the Peasant Family**, *Oxford 1983*

Weber, E: **Peasants into Frenchmen**, *London 1977*

VERNACULAR ARCHITECTURE

Chapelot, J and Fossier, R: **The Village and House in the Middle Ages**, *London 1980*

Doyon, G and Hubrecht R: **Architecture rurale et bourgeoise en France**, *Paris 1942*

Fontaine, R: **La maison de pays**, *Paris 1977*

Freal, J: **L'architecture paysanne en France**, *Paris 1977*

Gauthier, J-S: **Les maisons paysannes des vieilles provinces de France**, *Paris 1951*

Leron-Lesur, P: **Colombiers et pigeonniers en France**, *Paris 1985*

Maisons de nos campagnes (l'Ami des jardins et de la maison Special Number)

MEMOIRS & FICTION

Balzac, H de: **The Peasantry**, trans. E Marriage, *London l896*

Carles, E: **A Wild Herb Soup**, *London 1991*

Guillaumin, E: **The Life of a Simple Man**, *London 1983*

Hélias, P-J: **The Horse of Pride: life in a Breton village**, *London 1978*

Young, A: **Travels in France During the Years 1787-1790**; *London l889*

Zola, E: **The Earth**, Penguin Books, London 1989

Giono, J: **Regain**, *Paris 1930*

INTERIORS

Boulanger, G: **L'art de reconnaître les meubles régionaux**, *Paris 1966*

Gairaud, Y and Perthuis, F de: **Guide du meuble régional**, *Paris 1987*

Gauthier, J-S: **La connaissance des meubles régionaux français**, *Paris 1952*

Gauthier, J-S: **Le mobilier des vieilles provinces françaises**, *Paris 1958*

Langnon H and Huard, F: **French Provincial Furniture**, *Philadelphia 1927*

Oliver, L: **Reconnaître les styles régionaux**, *Paris ( )*

Reyniès, N de: **Le mobilier domestique**, 2 vols, *Paris 1987*

Styles régionaux: plaisirs de France, 4 vols, *Paris*

VERNACULAR ARCHITECTURE BY REGIONS

A number of books in this section are part of the series, L'architecture rurale francaise, designated ARF, and published under the auspices of the Musée Nationale des Arts et Traditions Populaires.

Alsace Lorraine

Denis, M-N and Groshens, M-C: **Alsace**, ARF, *Paris 1978*

Gérard, C: **Lorraine**, ARF, *Paris 1981*

Ruch, M and Gyss, J-P: **La maison traditionnelle d'Alsace**, *Paris 1986*

Auvergne

Breuille, P etc: **Maisons paysannes et vie traditionnelles en Auvergne**, Nonette 19( )

Marty, J-P: **Basse Auvergne, La maison rurale en Auvergne** (Les cahiers de construction traditionnelle), *Nonette 1978*

Ondet, R and Trapon, P: **Haute Auvergne, La maison rurale en Auvergne** (les cahiers de construction traditionnelle), *Nonette 1979*

Basque Country

Gallop, R: **A Book of the Basques**, *London 1930*

Loubergé, J: **La maison rurale en pays Basque** (Les cahiers de construction traditionnelle), *Nonette 1981*

Berry

Zarka, C: **Berry**, ARF, *Paris 1982*

Brittany

Hervé, P: **Maisons rurales de Bretagne**, *Morlaix 1981*

Le Couëdic, D le and Trochet, J-R: **Bretagne**, ARF, *Paris 1985*

Meirion-Jones, G: **The Vernacular Architecture of Brittany,** *Edinburgh 1982*

Pacqueteau, F: **Architecture et vie traditionnelle en Bretagne,** *Paris 1979*

Spence, K: **Brittany and the Bretons,** *London 1978*

Burgundy

Bucaille, R and Lévi-Strauss, L: **Bourgogne,** ARF, *Paris 1980*

Champagne

Imbault, D: **La Champagne: architecture régionale,** *Paris 1986*

Flanders & Picardy

Cuisenier, J; Raulin, H and Calame, F: **Nord Pas-de-Calais,** ARF, *Paris 1988*

Stein, A: **Le Nord** (La maison dans sa région) *Paris 1991*

Franche-Comté

Royer, C: **Franche-Comté,** ARF, *Paris 1977*

Guyenne & Gascony

Bidart, P and Collomb, G: **Pays Aquitains,** ARF, *Paris 1984*

Cayla, A: **Architecture paysanne de Guyenne et Gascogne,** *Paris 1977*

Ile de France

Billy-Christian, F de and Raulin, H: **Ile de France Orléanais,** ARF, *Paris 1986*

Vincent, M: **Maisons de Brie et d'Ile de France,** *Paris 1981*

Landes

Loubergé, J: **La maison rurale dans les Landes** (Les cahiers de construction traditionnelle), *Nonette 1982*

Toulgouat, P: **La vie rurale et la maison de l'ancienne lande,** *Pau 1987*

Languedoc, Rouergue and Cévennes

Cayla, A: **Architecture paysanne du Rouergue et Cévennes,** *Paris 1975*

Lhuisset, C: **L'architecture rurale en Languedoc, en Roussillon,** *Paris 1980*

Limousin

Robert, M; Boulanger, P; Guyot, F: **Les maisons limousines,** 'Ethnologia' (special number Autumn) *Limoges 1978*

Lyonnais

Royer, C: **Lyonnais,** ARF, *Paris 1979*

Midi-Pyrénées

Pawlowski, D and Fondevilla, H: **Vieilles maisons des pays d'oc; vol l: restaurer en pays toulousain,** *Toulouse 1980*

Rivals, C: **Midi-toulousain et pyrénéen,** ARF, *Paris 1979*

Normandy

Boithias, J-L and Mondin, C: **Haute Normandie, La maison rurale en Normandie** (Les cahiers de construction traditionnelle), *Nonette 1970*

Brier, M-A and Brunet, P: **Normandie,** ARF, *Paris 1984*

Brunet, P and Bertaux, J-J: **L'architecture rurale en Basse-Normandie,** *Museum of Normandy 1980*

Chaumely, J: **Styles de Normandie,** *Ciments Lafarge*

Déterville, P: **Manoirs du pays Auge,** *Condé-sur-Noireau 1982*

Freal, J: **Maisons de Normandie,** *Paris 1973*

Letenoux, G: **Architecture et vie traditionnelle en Normandie,** *Paris 1979*

Pays de Loire

Sarazin, A: **Fermes et logis du bocage de l'ouest: Anjou, Maine, Vendée;** *Paris 1975*

Périgord & Quercy

Cayla, A: **Maisons du Quercy et du Périgord,** *Paris 1973*

Simon, J-P: **L'architecture paysanne en Périgord et sa restauration,** *Paris 1991*

Poitou-Charentes

Suzanne, J: **Poitou, pays charentais,** ARF, *Paris 1981*

Provence

Bromberger, C; Lacroix, J; Raulin: H: **Provence,** ARF, *Paris 1980*

Perron, C: **Haute Provence habitée,** *Aix-en-Provence 1985*

Raybout, P and Perreard: **Comté de Nice,** ARF, *Paris 1982*

Savoy Dauphiné

Herman, M-T: **Architecture et vie traditionnelle en Savoie,** *Paris 1980*

Raulin, H: **Savoie,** ARF, *Paris 1977*

Raulin, H: **Dauphiné,** ARF, *Paris 1977*

MISCELLANEOUS

Ashurst, J: **Mortars, Plasters and Renders in Conservation,** *Aldershot 1988*

Durkan, A: **Vendange,** *London 1971*

Fillipetti H and Trotereau, J: **Symboles et pratiques rituelles dans la maison traditionelle,** *Paris 1978*

Jacquelin, L and Poulain, R: **The Wines and Vineyards of France,** *London 1965*

Thudichum, J: **A Treatise on Wines,** *London 1894*

INDEX

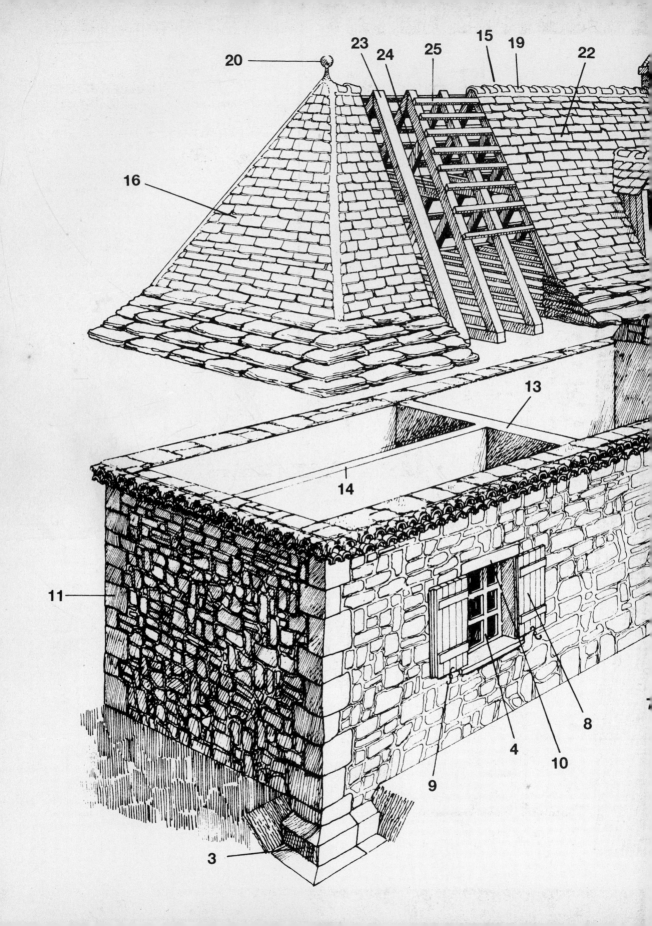